London International Conferences

PROCEEDINGS 2021-3

June 2021

London International Conferences, 3-5 June 2021, hosted online by UKEY Consulting and Publishing, London, United Kingdom

UKEY

CONSULTING & PUBLISHING

LONDONIC.UK

ISBN: 9798527104646

Proceeding: London International Conference, June 2021
Presenters:
A. Ayisha
A. Cekrezi
A. E. Pohan
A. Nasith
A. Sahrir
B. E. Alechenu
B. S. Agus Purwono
C. Schabasser
D. Rajan
E. A. Mammadov
E. Culfa
E. K. Sezgin
F. Nalcaci
H. M. Daulay
I. Asadov
I. E. Bisen
I. Kurt
P. Aurchana
I. Stasa
M. F. Tharaba
M. Jasin
O. Nosova
R. Malini
S. Alagappan
S. Prabavathy
S. Susan
Y. Polat
Y. Yildirim

Design: Studio Ima
Cover: Itaco
Publisher: UKEY Publishing
Version: V01
Series: Proceedings 03
Copyright © 2021 UKEY Publishing
ukeyconsultingpublishing.co.uk

ISBN: 9798527104646

Content

London International Conferences

londonic.uk

ukeyconsultingpublishing.co.uk

Communication Problems and Solutions in Family and Social Relationships

Ekrem Culfa
Mylife University
ekremculfa@gmail.com

Abstract

Communication, which has a great share in all the developments that have taken place since the beginning of its history and is still taking place, can cause great problems when used unhealthy.

Our communication mistakes that we ignore, ignore, ignore or simplify in today's conditions affect us a lot by causing the relations to break down completely and even an increase in hostility.

Failure to meet the most basic expectations both in our family-marriage life and in our bilateral relationships, in our friend groups and in our other social environment creates some wounds. It may be inevitable that the wounds caused by

London International Conferences, 3-5 June 2021, hosted online by UKEY Consulting and Publishing, London, United Kingdom

communication errors are reflected in the language during communication. In fact, this reflection in communications can lead to communicative failures, problems, showdowns and then some ruptures.

What are the basic communication problems in bilateral relations?

To find basic communication problems, let's focus on where the communication problem started and how it continues. Excitement is at its peak! Here's a tip: As we all know, our relationships often have a set of emotional responses that we expect. Is not it? Uh… or I can hear you say Yaaa Yeah. When we don't get these emotional responses that we expect from our partner or partner, there are two options; We either suppress our emotions or fight to get that answer. Our war to get what we want is expressed in communication; It can be reflected in a critical, responsible, accusatory, or even egocentric attitude. When an effort is made to identify the culprit and to show that he is right, two parties have already formed in the relationship automatically. However, love cannot be biased even if we want it. Two people who have decided to walk on the same road cannot be on different sides and separate fronts. This is where the beginning of miscommunication or unhealthy communication that can be dangerous for the relationship begins.

One of the basic rules of sustainable, healthy and ideal communication is to create a trust area. If our communication space is not secure, we immediately awaken a sense of alertness. This feeling prompts us to stay on the defensive or to deal with the feeling of not being understood.

Creating a safe space in the relationship starts with knowing that the other person is there willing to listen and understand us. If we want to have a healthy communication, we need to know that we will be understood and not judged during

London International Conferences, 3-5 June 2021, hosted online by UKEY Consulting and Publishing, London, United Kingdom

communication. Couples who provide this trust also need to show continuity in their communication in their relationships.

Where Are Technical Errors Done In Communication In Bilateral Relations?

The main mistakes made during communication can be listed as follows

Focusing on the past and continuously opening old books

Focusing on the past and constantly opening the old notebooks can bring about the repeated discussions of the problems that seem to be solved but not solved in fact. Thus, the couples put solving their actual problems to the second plan. As a result, this is nothing more than adding a new problem to the unresolved problems. Is not it? Just like I hear you say.

Being definitely, ignoring

There are a number of defensive mechanisms that each person uses specifically. To belittle, to ignore, to avoid and to ignore are a few of them. Evaluating the thoughts, feelings, and reactions in the face of any event, situation and attitude in relationships causes us to see the effect of the situation on our partner, and at the same time, we cannot provide the right communication and cause some communication accidents. Of course, there will be differences in thought, emotion and behavior patterns between partners, but empathizing will make it easier to understand and be understood, and it will show that the issue is not actually making a behavior, emotion or thought accepted by the other party, but only being listened to and understood by the partner in a healthy way.

Short and wall knitting

If you are offended or formally disrupt communication by building thick walls. Now you and your partner are dealing with an unsolved issue. In addition, you did not even leave a defense zone. What will we do in this situation? First of all,

London International Conferences, 3-5 June 2021, hosted online by UKEY Consulting and Publishing, London, United Kingdom

start by thinking about what this situation will give you. In this case, one or both sides may experience a feeling of guilt. Someone with a sense of guilt has a hard time realizing the full potential of what they can do for the relationship. Let's always keep this in the back of our minds, do not forget that when people feel safe by nature, they can work more easily.

Judgment by generalization, to cruise

Judging or blaming by generalizing puts the person into despair. It even causes him to see himself as inadequate and always like that.

On the other hand, when we talk about judgment and accusation while communicating, we have to accept that the person in front of us will listen not to understand us but to defend himself. When we come across accusation and judgment sentences, we immediately activate our primitive brain. While this situation causes us to break away from rational thinking and come under the control of emotions, anger and anger begin to dominate people. Thus, the results we need to draw from the incident may vary. However, communication is essential not what I understand, but what I am told.

Reading the brain

Finally, we can talk about a behavior that we can describe as trying to read the brain or thinking instead of others, which is a big problem. He doesn't love me anymore so he acts like this, he's angry with me and doesn't talk to me because he wants to punish me etc. Our behavior of trying to know the other person's true thoughts about us without knowing it...

In fact, if we want a healthy communication in the relationship, we should say stop to these references that we frequently refer to in our daily life. If, despite everything, you are experiencing communication or adjustment problems in

London International Conferences, 3-5 June 2021, hosted online by UKEY Consulting and Publishing, London, United Kingdom

your relationships, you should definitely seek professional help individually or as a couple.

Keywords: Communication problems, solutions in family, social relationships

London International Conferences, 3-5 June 2021, hosted online by UKEY Consulting and Publishing, London, United Kingdom

Musical Instruments Sound Classification using GMM

P. Aurchana
Department of Master of Computer Applications
Sri Manakula Vinayagar Engineering College
Puducherry, India

S. Prabavathy
Department of Computer Science
A. P. C. Mahalaxmi College for Women Thoothukudi
Tamilnadu, India

Abstract

Classification is the task of assigning objects to one of several predefined categories. In today's decade classifying the musical signal from large data is a major task; the proposed work classifies the music into their respective classes. In this paper, the sound of the musical instruments classified automatically from the musical signals. Mel frequency cepstral coefficient is used as a feature extractor and the machine learning model namely Gaussian Mixture Model is used for classification. This system tested in ten different classes of musical instrument sound from two different instrument families such as Woodwind and Brass instruments. In this

London International Conferences, 3-5 June 2021, hosted online by UKEY Consulting and Publishing, London, United Kingdom

proposed work, the result yields satisfactory accuracy in the classification of musical instruments sound.

Keywords: Musical Instrument Sound Classification (MISC), mel frequency cepstral coefficient (MFCC), Gaussian Mixture Model (GMM).

1. Introduction

Classification is more useful in the context of constructing vast audio collections that have been investigated, because the assigned class labels are directly displayed to the user and applied as a filter. As a result, it is used in an indirect way for music recommendation, where similarity may be determined for all labels based on advanced listening habits, and pick songs to listen to from the classes where a user has the most similarity. The task of automatically classifying the musical instruments is difficult. In the digital era, musical data classification has become a very prominent research topic. The classification of musical instruments was a lengthy manual process. This approach divides musical instruments into categories based on acoustic characteristics such as MFCC, Sonogram, and MFCC combined with Sonogram. The characteristics are classified using two modelling techniques: SVM and kNN. In this research, we use modern algorithms to classify musical instruments based on their attributes that are retrieved from diverse instruments. The suggested research compares and contrasts the performance of kNN and SVM. SVM and kNN classifiers are used to identify musical instruments and compute their accuracy [4].

Everyone in the present era listens to and plays music. Music is diverse all around the world. It is the fulcrum of all the arts and a language that speaks for itself. We might argue that this immaculate art's vast history extends to infinity and beyond. It would be more interesting if there was a method for us to learn about the instruments that are used in the song. As a result, may categorise music depending on certain instruments. Researchers have been actively involved in human perception towards the study of Musical Instruments for the past two decades [5].

London International Conferences, 3-5 June 2021, hosted online by UKEY Consulting and Publishing, London, United Kingdom

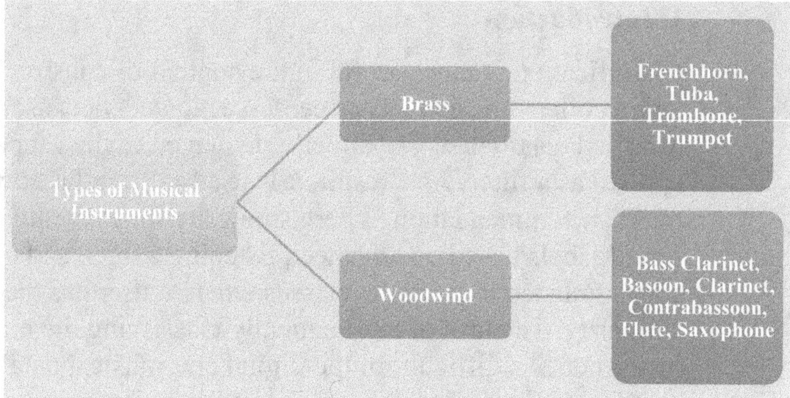

Fig. 1 Musical Instruments Types

In this proposed work, the musical instruments sound classification is done in three steps, first is the preprocessing of musical data, then the features are extracted and finally the classification process. Fig. 1 shows the types of musical instrument sound which is going to be categorized. The sound of the musical instruments used in this paper are French Horn, Tuba, Trombone, Trumpet from Brass and Bass Clarinet, Bassoon, Clarinet, Contrabassoon, Flute, Saxophone from Woodwind instrumentsFig.2 shows the proposed work of the system.

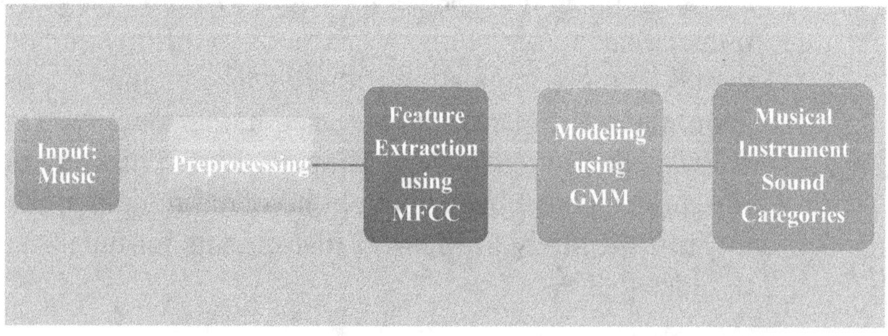

Fig. 2 Block diagram of the proposed work

London International Conferences, 3-5 June 2021, hosted online by UKEY Consulting and Publishing, London, United Kingdom

2. Review of Literature

Digital audio applications are already a common place aspect of our lives. Audio classification can be a useful method for managing content. If an audio clip can be automatically categorized, it may be saved in an organized database, greatly improving audio management. We present effective algorithms in this research for automatically classifying audio recordings into one of six categories: music, news, sports, advertisement, cartoon, and movie. To characterize the audio content for these categories, a number of acoustic features such as linear predictive coefficients, linear predictive cepstral coefficients, and mel-frequency cepstral coefficients are retrieved. The distribution of auditory feature vectors is captured using the Auto Associative Neural Network model (AANN). The AANN model captures the distribution of a class's acoustic features, and the weights of the network are adjusted using the backpropagation learning algorithm to minimise the mean square error for each feature vector. The suggested technique additionally compares the performance of AANN with that of a GMM, in which feature vectors from each class were utilized to train GMM models for those classes. The likelihood of a test sample belonging to each model is calculated during testing, and the sample is assigned to the class whose model produces the highest likelihood.

In music indexing, automatic music genre classification is quite useful. Tempogram is a feature extraction method based on the temporal structure of music data that is used in the classification of musical genres. The major aspects of today's music genre classification system are searching and arranging. This research describes a new methodology for classifying music that employs support vector machines. The Gaussian mixture model learns from training data to classify music audio into its appropriate categories. The suggested feature extraction and classification methods improve music genre classification accuracy [2].

London International Conferences, 3-5 June 2021, hosted online by UKEY Consulting and Publishing, London, United Kingdom

This research provides a unique feature extraction approach based on Fractional Fourier Transform (FrFT)-based Mel Frequency Cepstral Coefficient (MFCC) characteristics for autonomous musical instrument categorization. The proposed system's classifier model was created using a Counter Propagation Neural Network (CPNN). When compared to other traditional features, the proposed features' discriminating capability has been maximised for between-class instruments and minimised for within-class instruments. In addition, when compared to other conventional features, the proposed features show a significant improvement in classification accuracy and robustness against Additive White Gaussian Noise (AWGN). The sound database from McGill University Master Sample (MUMS) was utilised to evaluate the system's performance [3].

To solve the challenge of music instrument recognition, speech and audio processing techniques are combined with statistical pattern recognition concepts. The suggested approach is scalable from isolation notes to solo instrumental phrases without the necessity for temporal segmentation of solo music because only non temporal, frame level information are utilized. Line Spectral Frequencies (LSF) are presented as features for music instrument recognition based on their usefulness in speech. MFCC and LPCC features have also been used to evaluate the proposed system and for classification, Gaussian Mixture Models (GMM) and the K-Nearest Neighbor (KNN) model are utilized. The experimental dataset includes databases from the University of Iowa's MIS and the C Music Corporation's RWC. When identifying 14 musical instruments, the best scores were around 95% at the musical instrument family level and 90% at the musical instrument level [10].

3. Preprocessing

A musical audio signal preprocessing takes place is as follows. Pre-emphasis, segmentation, and windowing are the steps in the preprocessing of raw musical data. The original music signal is first pre-processed, with the main purpose of unifying the music format, applying pre-emphasis, and segmenting the musical signal. Windowing and framing are then applied to all audio parts of the music.

3.1 Preemphasis

The digitized music signal is processed through a low order digital system to spectrally flatten it and make it less sensitive to fixed precision effects later in the music signal processing. It is usual practice to use the first order difference equation to preemphasis the music signal.

$$s'_n = s_n - k\, s_n - 1 \tag{1}$$

to the samples {sn, n = 1, N} in each window. Here k is the preemphasis coefficient which should be in the range $0 \leq k < 1$.

3.2 Frame blocking

The continuous music signal is then divided into N frames of musical audio samples, with neighbouring frames separated by M (M < N). The first N audio samples make up the first frame. After the first frame, the second frame starts with M samples and overlaps it with N - M samples, and so on. This process is repeated until all of the music data is accounted for one or more frames. A frame rate of 160 frames per second is employed throughout this paper, with each frame lasting 20 milliseconds and a 50% overlap between subsequent frames. Fig. 3 depicts the overall process, which displays the sampled audio waveform being converted into a sequence of parameter blocks. The waveform segment used to determine each parameter vector is commonly referred to as a window, and the volume of the window is referred to as the window size. Frame rate and window size are unrelated. In general, the window size will be larger than the frame rate, causing succeeding windows to overlap.

3.3 Windowing

Finally, tapering the samples in each window to reduce discontinuities at the window's edges is beneficial. It performs the following transformation on the samples in the window sn, n = 1,N

$$s'_n = \left\{ 0.54 - 0.46 \cos\left(\frac{2\pi(n-1)}{N-1}\right) \right\} s_n \qquad (2)$$

In practice, all the above three steps are typically followed.

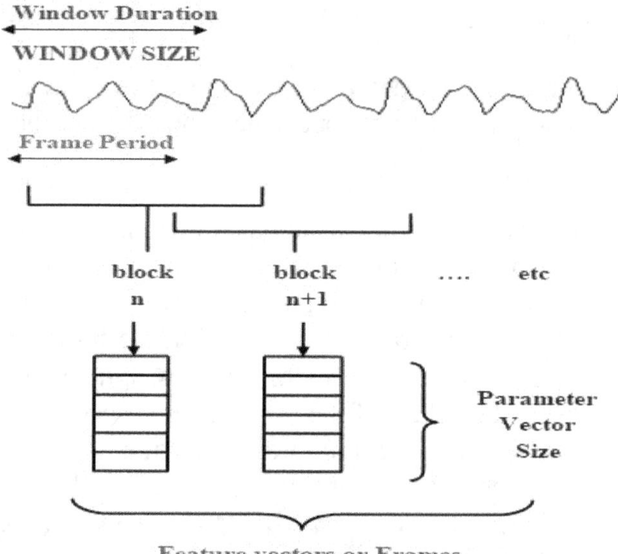

Fig. 3 Frame blocking

4. Feature Extraction Techniques

London International Conferences, 3-5 June 2021, hosted online by UKEY Consulting and Publishing, London, United Kingdom

Once the music signal gets preprocessed, MFCC features are extracted.

Mel frequency Cepstral Coefficients

In the area of music, audio and speech processing the Mel frequency Cepstral Coefficients (MFCC) are the short-term spectral features that are commonly used. The mel frequency cepstrum has been shown to be extremely effective at identifying the composition of musical audio signals as well as modelling the subjective frequency and pitch content of those signals.

The MFCCs have been used in a variety of sound mining activities and have demonstrated superior performance when compared to other features. MFCC was calculated in a variety of ways by different writers. As a result, the goal of this research is to figure out how many coefficients are appropriate for sound classification of musical instruments. The MFCC features are employed to analyse the musical instrument signal in this study.

The phonetically important elements of audio, music, and speech are captured using MFCCs, which are based on the well-known change of the human ear's essential bandwidths with frequency, logarithmically at high frequencies and linearly at low frequencies. The musical audio signals are segmented and windowed into short frames of 20 ms to obtain MFCCs. Figure 1 shows a block diagram for extracting MFCC features. in Fig 4.

London International Conferences, 3-5 June 2021, hosted online by UKEY Consulting and Publishing, London, United Kingdom

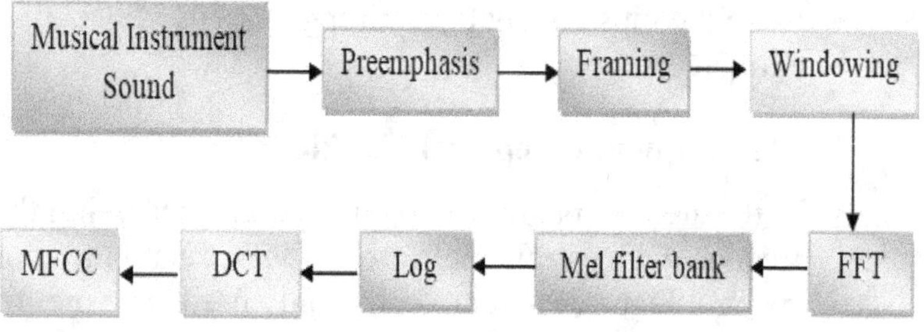

Fig. 4 Extraction the MFCC features from Music Signal

Mel frequency wrapping

For each of these frames, the magnitude spectrum is calculated using the Fast Fourier Transform (FFT) and converted into a collection of outputs from the mel scale filter bank. The filter bank analysis makes obtaining the appropriate non-linear frequency resolution a lot easier. Filter bank amplitudes, on the other hand, are highly correlated, making the employment of a cepstral transformation nearly mandatory in this scenario. On a mel-scale, a simple Fourier transform based filter bank is designed to provide about equivalent resolution.

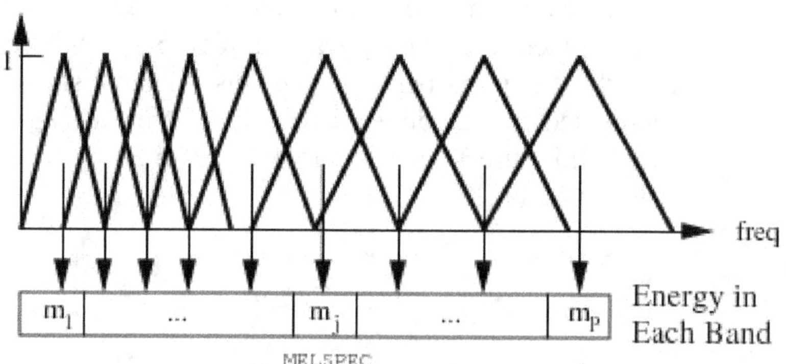

Fig. 5 Mel scale filter bank

London International Conferences, 3-5 June 2021, hosted online by UKEY Consulting and Publishing, London, United Kingdom

Fig. 5 illustrates the general structure of this filter bank. As can be seen, the filters used are triangular and they are equally spaced along the mel-scale which is defined by

$$Mel(f) = 2595\ln\left(1 + \frac{f}{700}\right) \tag{3}$$

To create this filter bank, a Fourier transform is applied to a window of musical audio data, and the magnitude is calculated. By correlating the magnitude coefficients with the complete triangle filter, the magnitude coefficients are then binned. In this case, binning implies multiplying each FFT magnitude coefficient by the relevant filter grow and collecting the results. As a result, each bin contains a weighted sum that represents the spectral magnitude in that filter bank channel.

Triangular filters are often stretched across the entire frequency range from zero to Nyquist frequency. Band-limiting, on the other hand, is frequently used to reject undesired frequencies or avoid assigning filters to frequency zones with no useful signal energy. Lower and upper frequency cut-offs can be specified for filter bank analysis. The stated number of filter bank channels are spread evenly on the mel-scale over the resulting pass-band when low and high pass cut-offs are adjusted in this manner.

Cepstrum

To obtain the MFCCs, the logarithm is applied to the filter bank outputs, followed by Discrete Cosine Transformation (DCT). Because the mel spectrum coefficients (and their logarithms) are real numbers, the DCT can be used to transform them to the time domain. In practice, for computing efficiency, the final step of inverse Discrete Fourier Transform (DFT) is replaced by DCT. For the stated frame analysis, the cepstral representation of the music spectrum provides a superior representation of the signal's nearby spectral features. The first 13 MFCCs are typically used as features [6] [7].

At the segmental level, 12 MFCC coefficients (c_1, c_2, c_3, …, c_{12}) for each frame are retrieved from the musical audio signal. The DCT excludes the 'null' MFCC coefficient c_0, which represents the mean value of the input musical audio stream, which contains minimal information. Dynamic parameters generated from 13th order static cepstral coefficients (c_0, c_1, c_2, c_3, …, c_{12}) have been proposed and proved to improve audio categorization system performance. The delta-cepstrum (first-order difference of the short-time static cepstrum), the delta-delta-cepstrum (second-order difference of the static cepstrum), and delta- and delta-delta-energy are examples of dynamic characteristics. In noisy environments, dynamic features have been shown to be more durable than static features. The dynamic and static aspects of a musical audio signal spectrum with 13th order static coefficients, 13th order delta coefficients, and 13th order acceleration (delta-delta) coefficients are captured using a 39th order MFCC. For each frame, this yields a 39-dimensional MFCC feature vector.

The MFCC features are extracted as described for ten categories of sound of the musical instruments namely Bass Clarinet, Bassoon, Clarinet, Contrabassoon, Flute, French Horn, Saxophone, Trombone, Trumpet, and Tuba respectively.

5. Modeling the Features

Gaussian Mixture Model

Parametric or nonparametric approaches are used to model the probability distribution of feature vectors. Parametric models are those that assume the shape of a probability density function. In nonparametric modelling, the probability distribution of feature vectors is assumed to be minimum or nonexistent. The Gaussian mixing model (GMM) is briefly discussed in this section. The rationale for employing GMM is that a mixture of Gaussian densities can be used to describe the distribution of feature vectors derived from a class, as illustrated in Fig. 6.

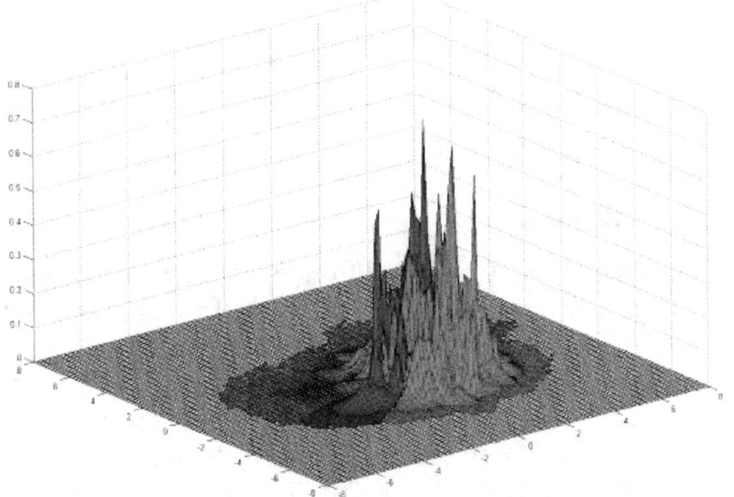

Fig. 6 Gaussian Mixture Model

GMMs use Gaussian components to describe feature vectors and are defined by the mean vector and co-variance matrix [8]. GMM models have the potential to construct an arbitrary shaped observation density even in the absence of other information [9].

6. Performance Measures

This study used a set of assessment metrics, including Accuracy, Precision, Recall, and F-score, to assess the performance of the classifier GMM using MFCC. The confusion matrix, which is obtained from the classification process's output, is used to determine these metrics. The confusion matrix is a 2 x 2 matrix with four elements: True Positive (TP), True Negative (TN), False Positive (FP), and False Negative (FN), where TP indicates that the prediction is correct, TN indicates that the prediction is incorrect, FP indicates that the correct value is predicted incorrectly, and FN indicates that the wrong value is predicted correctly.

7. Experimental Results

7.1. Dataset

The data was collected from the online musical database Instrument Recognition in Musical Audio Signals (IRMAS). Bass Clarinet, Bassoon, Clarinet, Contrabassoon, Flute, French Horn, Saxophone, Trombone, Trumpet, and Tuba were among the 1000 musical audio clips. Each clip contains music data with a duration ranging from 1 to 10 seconds, sampled at 8 kHz and encoded in 16-bit. For training, 800 musical audio data samples were employed, and 200 for testing. For further implementation, the music clips are preprocessed using pre-emphasis, segmentation, and windowing.

7.2. Acoustic Feature Extraction

Fixed-length and overlapping frames are created from the training data (in our work 20 ms frames with 10 ms overlapping). The temporal features of music data can be processed in the training phase when the surrounding frames are overlapped. Because of the 8 kHz sampling rate, 20 ms frames contain 160 values. These 160 values are translated into 39 MFCC coefficients, each of which represents a single frame. For 1 second of music data, there are 100 such frames. For each of the ten categories, the feature extraction method is performed for musical audio samples of varied durations such as 1 second, 3 seconds, 5 seconds, and 10 seconds.

Experiments are carried out to test acoustic feature MFCC, as well as the performance of GMM.

7.3. Gaussian Mixture Model

Gaussian mixtures for the ten classes are modeled for the MFCC feature. For classification the feature vectors are extracted and each of the feature vector is given as input to the GMM model. The distribution of the acoustic features are captured using GMM. We have chosen a mixture of 1, 3, 5, 10 mixture models. Audio classification using GMM gives an accuracy of 86.98%. The performance of GMM for different mixtures as shown in Fig. 7 shows the accuracy of different data durations, the best performance was achieved with 10 Gaussian mixtures compared to the other mixtures. Fig. 8 shows the performance of GMM for musical audio classification.

Table 1 Overall accuracy of GMM with MFCC

Model	1 second	2 seconds	3 seconds	10 seconds
GMM	86.90	84.11	88.24	89.35

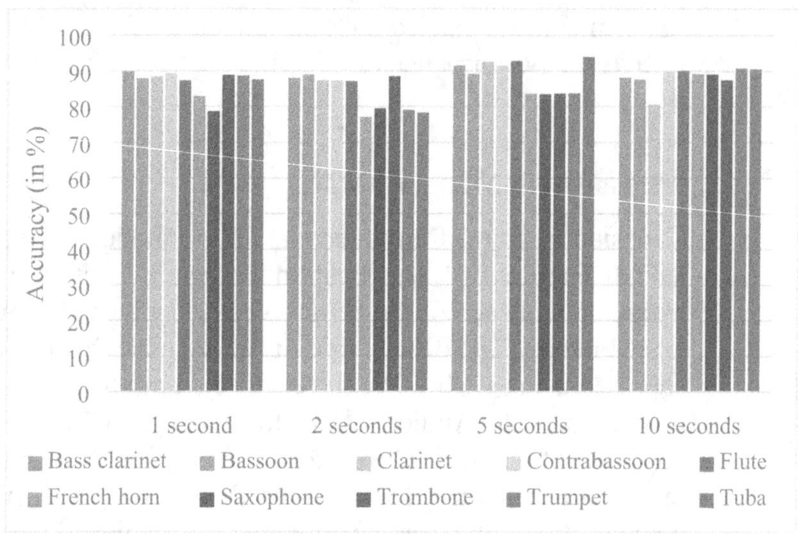

Fig. 7 Accuracy of the proposed system for various duration

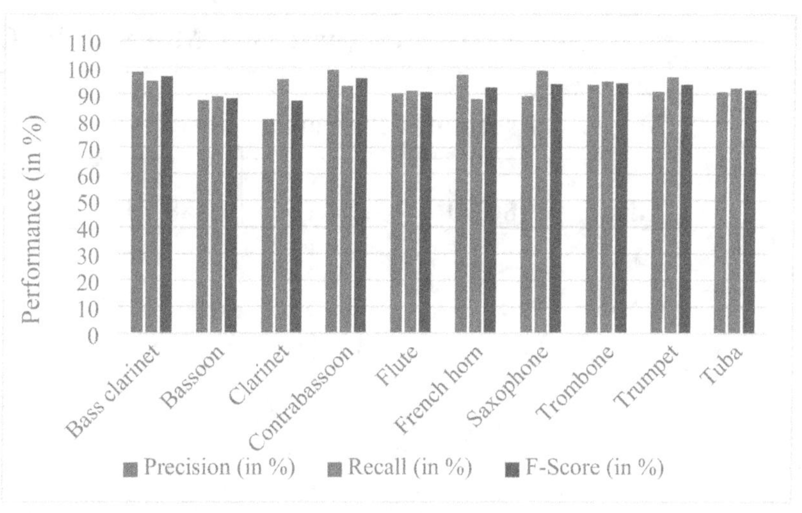

Fig. 8 Performance of the proposed work

8. Conclusion

In this work, a GMM classifier with MFCC features used to classify musical instrument sounds automatically. The performance of GMM yields a satisfactory accuracy of 86.98 %. When compared to 1 second, 3 seconds, and 5 seconds data the 10 seconds data provides the maximum accuracy from the training data. The sound classification model for musical instruments will be updated in the future to discriminate more classes.

London International Conferences, 3-5 June 2021, hosted online by UKEY Consulting and Publishing, London, United Kingdom

9. References

[1] Dhanalakshmi, P., Palanivel, Sengottayan & Ramalingam, Vivekanandan. (2011). Classification of audio signals using AANN and GMM. *Applied Soft Computing*. 11. Pp. 716-723, 10.1016/j.asoc.2009.12.033.

[2] Thiruvengatanadhan, R., Music Genre Classification using GMM (2018). *International Research Journal of Engineering and Technology (IRJET)*, Volume: 05 Issue: 10.

[3] Bhalke, D.G., Rao, C.B.R. & Bormane, D.S. Automatic Musical Instrument Classification using Fractional Fourier Transform based- MFCC features and Counter Propagation Neural Network. *J Intell Inf Syst* 46, 425–446 (2016). https://doi.org/10.1007/s10844-015-0360-9

[4] Prabavathy, S, Rathikarani, V., & Dhanalakshmi, P, Classification of Musical Instruments using SVM and KNN, *International Journal of Innovative Technology and Exploring Engineering (IJITEE)*, ISSN: 2278-3075, Volume-9 Issue-7, May 2020.

[5] Shreevathsa, P. K., Harshith, M., A. R. M. & Ashwini, "Music Instrument Recognition using Machine Learning Algorithms," 2020 *International Conference on Computation, Automation and Knowledge Management (ICCAKM)*, 2020, pp. 161-166, doi: 10.1109/ICCAKM46823.2020.9051514.

[6] Dhanalakshmi, P. (2010). *Classification of Audio for Retrieval Applications*. [Doctoral Dissertation]. Faculty of Computer Science and Engineering, Annamalai University, Chidambaram, Tamilnadu.

[7] Zokaee, Sara & Faez, Karim. (2012). *Human Identification Based on Electrocardiogram and Palmprint*. 2. 261-266.

[8] Rafael Iriya & Miguel Arjona Ramírez. Gaussian Mixture Models with Class-Dependent Features for Speech Emotion Recognition. *IEEE Workshop on Statistical Signal Processing,* pp. 480-483, 2014.

[9] Tang, H., Chu, S. M., Hasegawa-Johnson, M. & Huang, T. S., Partially Supervised Speaker Clustering. *IEEE transactions on Pattern Analysis and Machine Intelligence.* vol. 34, no. 5, pp. 959-971, 2012.

[10] Krishna, A.G. & Sreenivas, Tv. (2004). Music instrument recognition: from isolated notes to solo phrases. *International Conference on Acoustics, Speech, and Signal Processing,* ICASSP.

London International Conferences

londonic.uk

ukeyconsultingpublishing.co.uk

International Visitors Gastronomy Behaviors And Expectations: Aydin Province Model

Emrah Köksal Sezgin
ekoksalsezgin@gmail.com

Abstract

This research includes findings and interpretations aiming to determine theoretical information on gastronomy tourism and international visitors' gastronomy behaviors and expectations in terms of Aydın province model. The problem sentence of the research in which Aydın province's gastronomic properties are aimed to be determined and the fulfillment level of the international visitors' gastronomy behaviors and expectations are aimed to be measured accordingly has been determined as: "what is the fulfillment level of the international visitors' gastronomy preferences and expectations within the scope of Aydın province gastronomic properties?". Along with this general problem sentence, other sub-problems have been tried to be replied as well. The first stage of the research was completed with a questionnaire applied to tourists staying in Kuşadası in order to determine the preferences and expectations of the tourists who visited the region. At the

London International Conferences, 3-5 June 2021, hosted online by UKEY Consulting and Publishing, London, United Kingdom

second stage of the research, a semi-structured interview form was applied to the participants in order to determine Aydın province's gastronomic properties from a qualitative point of view. At the third stage of the research, international food festival attendants were requested to make an assessment on the menu which reflects the gastronomic properties of Aydın province through the assessment form of the World Association of Chefs' Societies with the intention of assessment of the determined gastronomic properties of the province.

Keywords: International visitors, gastronomy behavior, gastronomy tourism, Aydın, Turkey

London International Conferences, 3-5 June 2021, hosted online by UKEY Consulting and Publishing, London, United Kingdom

Impact of Migration on Personal Portrait of Migrants

R. Malini

PG Department of Commerce and Research Centre,
Sri Parasakthi College for Women, Courtallam
maliniramu@yahoo.co.in

A. Ayisha

PG Department of Commerce and Research Centre,
Sri Parasakthi College for Women, Courtallam
bmrayishababu@gmail.com

Abstract

The home and homeland of every living being is the safe and secure place to live in. In order to uphold their standard of living, people emigrate from their country and immigrate to other countries. The standard of living largely endorsed by personal portrait of migrants. This phenomenon induces the researchers to analyse the impact of migration on personal portraits of the migrants in pre and post migration. The analysis done on the basis of primary data collected from 520 Indian Muslim Migrants from Tamil Nadu by adopting snow

London International Conferences, 3-5 June 2021, hosted online by UKEY Consulting and Publishing, London, United Kingdom

ball non- probability sampling. The responses of migrants regarding their self portrait before and after migration tested with the help of paired "t" test. The notable changes have been identified in migrants' Personal Grooming, Communication, Preference of Food, Eating Habit and Smartness. Besides, the result revealed that migrants' looked their unhealthy behaviour such as smoking, consuming of alcohol and drugs as habits. The migrants should strengthen the positive impact on self portrait to heal self and become the best human capital for the home land and the country they live...Besides, they should wane their unhealthy behaviour to become role model for the potential migrants of homeland.

Keywords: **impact of migration, migrants, personal portrait.**

1. Introduction

Migration is moving from one place to another to enhance the living and working condition. Movement of people from their home to another city, state or country for job, shelter or some other reasons is called migration. Most immigrants to Gulf countries stay, establish a living and earn money in the country. Despite cultural conflicts, language barriers, marginalization, most immigrants continue to find that Gulf countries are a land with more opportunity than their homeland, and they draw on all their tangible and intangible resources to survive here. For decades political and financial pressures have forced generations of educated Indian Muslims to leave their homes and travel as economic migrants in search of a better future overseas. Human migration is a physical movement of human beings either as individuals or as groups from one place to another place for innumerable causes. These migrations are not new and since time immemorial, the human beings have been shifting from one place to another as families, tribes, hordes and other forms of social groups for food, shelter, security and other reasons. When investigating something in personal portraits of before and after the process of people's migration to gulf countries. Migratory flows are generally organized to meet immediate needs and solve latent socio-economic tension though it might be for the uplifting a particular class. The positive impact is that the rural class will advance through migration. There will be the welfare of the rural class and it will lead to their social-cultural transformation and development. This is the most important impact of migration on personal portraits that it separates an individual from his place of origin and adds him to the place of destination. The purpose of settling down, commonly known as migration and it has been a universal phenomenon.

The home and homeland of every living being is the safe and secure place to live in. In order to uphold their standard of

London International Conferences, 3-5 June 2021, hosted online by UKEY Consulting and Publishing, London, United Kingdom

living, people emigrate from their country and immigrate to other countries. The standard of living largely endorsed by personal portrait of migrants. This phenomenon induces the researchers to analyse the impact of migration on personal portraits of the migrants in pre and post migration. The Impact of migration on personal portraits can be analysed by applying paired' test for pre and post migration. Data are often summarized by giving their mean and standard deviation and the paired' test is used to compare the means of the two samples of related data. The paired' test compares the mean difference, the standard deviation of the difference and the number of cases. Various explanations made on the basis of personal interview with migrants while collecting the data. The migrants' Personal Portrait of pre and post migration regarding Dressing Sense, Personal Grooming, Communication, Preference of Food, Eating Habit, Smartness, Habit of Smoking, Habit of Alcohol /Drug and Brand Preference are assessed.

2. Significance of the study

This paper will focus on the practical aspects of personal portraits that desire to draw forth and represent the self. Such a psychological exploration will lead us into the marvellous variety of personal portrait experiences. When investigating something in personal portraits. A subject looking outside the frame of the image, towards someone or something, suggests a presence external to the image that distracts the viewer's attention from the subject's presence Varieties of Self-Portrait. The migrants' personal portrait represents how he sees himself, what he is feeling, and how he wants to be seen by others.

The research methodology of this study will be a mode/ model to the potential research scholars to design their present/ future research. Further it will serve as a strong source of secondary data for the academicians and scholars to pursue their research.

3. Statistical Significance of the Study

Indian population is almost spread all over the world and make significant Diasporas in the world after China. According to the latest estimate by MOIA, Indian emigrants (both PIO and NRI) constituted about 30 million in 130 countries. The data was collected from various national and international documents such as MOIA (Ministry of Overseas Indian Affairs), ILO (Indian Labour Organization), IOM (International Organization of Migration), and United Nations reports on the workers' rights and so on. The Table No.1, the pie diagram and Table No. 2 below are representative of the data from the above mentioned organisations.

Table 1. Details of Indian Migrants in Other Countries During (2015-16)

Sl.No.	Country	Number of Indian Migrants	% contribution based on 2015 numbers
1	Saudi Arabia	2,800,000	24.6%
2	UAE	2,630,000	17.6%
3	USA	1,272,846	11.2%
4	Kuwait	758,615	6.7%
5	Oman	707,850	6.2%
6	Nepal	600,000	5.3%
7	Qatar	600,000	5.3%
8	Bahrain	350,000	3.1%
9	Singapore	350,000	3.1%
10	New Zealand	45,000	0.4%
11	Australia	251,000	2.2%
12	Canada	184,320	1.6%
13	Germany	43,000	0.4%
14	UK	325,000	2.9%
15	Malaysia	150,000	1.3%
16	Sri Lanka	14,000	0.1%
17	South Africa	50,000	0.4%
18	Netherlands	20,000	0.2%
19	Ethiopia	10,000	0.1%
20	Uganda	25,000	0.2%
21	Other (186)	823,115	7.2%

	Total	11,379,746	100.0%

Source: MOIA

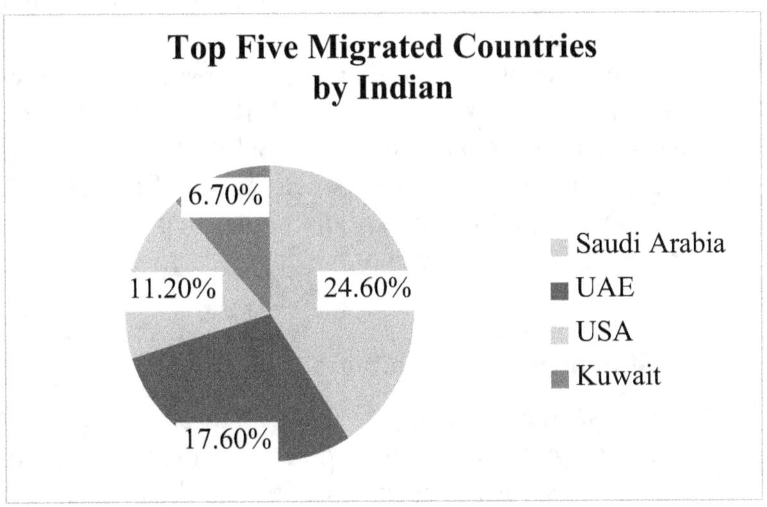

Figure 1. Details of Migration from Southern States of India

TABLE 2. Migration from Southern States of India

States	Emigration Clearance
Kerala	66058
Andhra Pradesh	53104
Telangana	38531
Tamil Nadu	83202

Source: MOIA

With special reference to the Table No.2, the Indian Muslim
Migrants from four different states of India who work across
seas are taken into survey. The Gulf region has enjoyed a

tremendously sustained growth in productivity over the last three decades. A major factor behind this productivity has been the easy availability of an educated, skilled and at the snare time, cheap workforce. The reason for this easy availability is the Gulf region's proximity to talent-rich regions like the Indian subcontinents. Indians have constituted about 60 percent of the workforce in the Gulf of which 40 percent are Muslims especially who belong to Tamil Nadu. Comparatively, the Muslims Migrants of Tamil Nadu who are overseas seem to be drastically higher than that of the other states of India. In this context, the research work is undertaken.

4. Statement of the Problem

This research work aims to make an in-depth study by addressing the various issues that come across in the life of migrants. Some people may depend on their agricultural lands in vain; some may search for a job and fails to find one because of poor education or lack of opportunities in this competitive world; some other people may suffer a lot to manage their family needs because of a less paid job. These are some of the criteria under which the people are forced to be the victims and they try their level best searching for appreciable opportunities overseas. Through this analysis Impact of migration on Personal Portraits are being looked upon; the very first factor starts with the Dressing Sense, Personal Grooming, Communication, Preference of food, Eating Habit, Smartness, Habit of smoking, Habit of Alcohol / Drug, and Brand preference. Through this analysis certain factors of this variety are being looked upon; the very first factor starts with.

- Is there any Impact in Personal Portrait of migrants due to migration to Gulf Countries?
- Is there any significant change in the Personal Portrait of pre and post migration of the Migrants?

5. Review of Literature

The inclusive study and interpretation of literature that relates to the present study plays a vital role in providing an insight into the research. Hence, the research work pursued from 2014 to 2019 related to this study were reviewed and given below.

Kumari (2014)1 made an attempt on —Rural- Urban migration in India: Determinants and factors‖. The research paper aims to study on rural-urban migration arising out of various social, economic or political reasons. The main purpose of the study was to find the significant economic factors responsible for the variations in the level of rural-urban migration and whether NREGA Act (2005) could have an impact on the rural migration in India on the basis of secondary data. In methodology, secondary data analysis such as ‗F' test, standard deviation, and other statistical methods were used to explain the results of the study. The present study discussed the data on migration in India, which was extracted from the National Sample Survey Organization (NSSO) during 2007-08 and census data during 2011. The study found that a rapid increase in internal migration in India. While discussing migration rate, it was found that the migration rate in urban areas (35 percent) was far higher than in rural areas (26 percent). Among the migrants in the rural areas, nearly 91 percent had migrated from rural areas and 8 percent from urban areas, whereas among the migrants in the urban areas, 59 percent had migrated from rural areas and 40 percent from urban areas. Hence MNREGA employment programmes were not contributed towards rural –urban migration. The study suggest that migration is essential for development and it is a desirable phenomenon; but what is not desirable is the distressed migration found across the nation resulting in over-crowding of cities. But there exists some social factors apart from such economic factors which also play an important role in explaining the nature and stream of rural- urban migration. The study concludes that it is possible only when the government's policies for the development in rural areas, and the nature of mass migration can be more helpful in rooting out the problem and seeking out the solution for the policy makers for the bright future of rural India.

Chandrasekhar and Sharma (2015)2 did research entitled"Urbanization and spatial patterns of internal migration in India". The research paper focuses on the issues of urbanization and internal migration in the context of India. The paper is important to highlight these aspects at the outset since urbanization is synonymous with non agricultural activities. The two sets of secondary data analysis was done on the basis of Census of India, 2001 and 2011 data, National Sample Survey Organisation (NSSO) 1983, 1987-88, 1999-2000 and 2007-08 data. Survey of Employment and Unemployment were utilized and described for internal migration. It is found that urban areas increased from 27.81 to 31.16 percent in the period of 2001-2011 and size of per urban areas also increased among the total population in urban 22.2 percent from the rural to urban migration and also it is found that internal migration patterns and its emerging trends, migration flow across states in India, the phenomenon of commuting and return migration had been increased from 5.4 to 10.9 percent in last decade, it was failed to understand, how migration affects well-being of individual at the source of destination. The study suggests that the event of expansion in nonfarm employment opportunities and growth in the agro-processing industries, the fastest urban growth could occur in small cities and towns. Rural–urban migrants might gravitate towards such cities and towns. This indicates an urgent need to formulate policy aimed at helping small cities, towns and large rural centres become vibrant centres of growth. The study concludes that there is a need to develop methods for estimating urban growth and migration simultaneously. Educated migrant workers were engaged in skilled labour and less educated workers were engaged in low paid work and kept on migrating from one place to another. Hence, the onus is on the demographers to utilize the available data sets and improve on the methods currently used for modelling rural–urban migration and forecasting city growth rates.

Sasi and Santha (2017)3 discussed the characteristics of —Immigrant labourers in Perumbavoor‖ (Kerala).The study aims to analyse the characteristics of migrant labourers in Perumbavoor. For this analysis, statistical tools like percentages, chi-square test and correlation coefficient were used. The respondents of the study consist of migrant labourers from different states of India who came to work in Perumbavoor at present. The data were suitably classified and analyzed based on the objective of the study. It was found that 58 percent of the respondents had stayed 30 years in the city, equal percent (58.0%) had stayed in a single room, 70 percent had used a common toilet, and 68 percent had cooked in a common room. The null hypotheses that there was no significant relationship between 55 the daily wages of the respondents and their monthly remittance to home was rejected by the study. The study reported that the peer group informed their responses regarding employment opportunities. The scholars had conducted another study about the problems of immigrant workers in Perumbavoor town. Around 40 percent respondents faced difficulty in payment, 34 percent respondents bought house, 30 percent respondents were based on finance, and 40 percent faced family problems. They also faced the problem of medical services and holiday or leaves at the time of need. It is found that most of the respondents faced housing problems, difficulties with their salaries and serious financial problems. Some of them faced serious family problems and difficulties in finding jobs. The main institutional help obtained by respondents was from the

London International Conferences, 3-5 June 2021, hosted online by UKEY Consulting and Publishing, London, United Kingdom

Government and bank. Most of the respondents were getting medical help at emergencies. The study suggests that migration causes changes in the distribution of jobs, income and economic resources in both the sending and receiving regions, and thus, structural transformation of rural and urban economy. Neither the social and cultural impacts of migration can be under looked. The study concludes that most of the respondents raised funds from parents and relatives to reach Kerala. Construction, trade and manufacturing are the main sectors of working by the respondents. More than half of the respondents were unskilled workers most of the respondents faced housing problems, difficulties with their salaries and serious financial problems. A few faced serious family problems and difficulties in finding jobs.

Ali et al. (2017)[3] analysed the topic "Gender differentials in inter-state out-migration in India". This study intend to look at the change in the level of employment related inter- state out migration in India and this study brings out the change occurred in the rate of inter- state out migration between 1993 and 2007-2008. The secondary data was collected with the help of statistical information of NSSO Report 1993 and 2007-2008. For this analysis, statistical tool like multivariate analysis in terms of logistic regression has been used. In order to examine the association between household socio- economic conditions with migration status the researcher have used multivariate binary logistic regression model. It revealed two times increase in interstate out-migration between1993 to 2007. During this period, migration occurred among the vast majority among 80 percent female migrates because of marriage and its related causes. Total migration rate in India is 23 (Per 1000 population) and in Karnataka 11.3% Chandigarh had highest female out-migration i.e., 31.7% and Assam had lowest female out-migration i.e., 1.8% and Karnataka State has 11.3% female out-migrates. It is also found that migration probability consistently decreases for people of higher

London International Conferences, 3-5 June 2021, hosted online by UKEY Consulting and Publishing, London, United Kingdom

expenditure quintiles with reference to the people of the lowest quintile and also it is found that women in India have less likelihood of being interstate out-migrants than males. This paper finds a two times increase in inter-state out- migration in India during last one and a half decades. This study shows that the adjusted employment related reason of migration for inter-state women rises to 18 per cent at the all India level. The logistic regression analysis further shows that these women who reported marriage a reason of migration but actually part of the workforce belong to lower socio-economic households. The study suggests that more than 3.5 times of the number of women migrated for employment are in a way economic migrants within those women who actually reported marriage as the reason for their marriage. The study felt that female migration in India impacted on the development and growth of the multidimensional fabric of the Indian society. As a concluding remark, from the increasing volume of internal out-migration across the states/union territories, it may not be correct to hold the view that Indian people are still adamant to migrate. At the same time there are reasons to hold the view of male prerogatives in migration. Hence, there is a need to change our mind-set to appreciate that the women migration is a positive process and they have also right to migrate internally and internationally and women's inter-state migration has also affirmative impact on key aspects of development and growth and they can enrich the multidimensional fabric of the Indian society.

Hendriks et al. (2018)5 studied the —Unsuccessful subjective well being assimilation among immigrants‖. The researcher aims to contribute to filling this void in the literature on migrant well-being by theorizing and exploring the extent to which —and under what conditions—faltering perceptions of the host country's societal conditions are associated with the subjective well-being assimilation of immigrants in developed European countries over time and across generations. This paper additionally investigates how differences in societal perceptions between natives and immigrants affect the immigrant-native gap in subjective well-being. The Qualitative and quantitative data analysis was done by using bi-annual European Social Survey cross-sectional, and multi-country data taken from the period of 2010–2016. The analysis sample includes respondents residing in 17 developed European countries, the researcher show that the gradual development of less positive perceptions of the host country's economic, political, and social conditions is associated with less positive subjective well-being trajectories among first generation immigrants and across migrant generations in developed European countries. The analysis is divided into four Hypotheses. The researcher test Hypothesis: by exploring how the changing societal perceptions of first-generation migrants relate to their subjective well-being development, by exploring the extent to which the mediating role of changing societal perceptions is conditional on various migrant characteristics, by exploring how societal perceptions relate to the subjective well-being assimilation of second generation immigrants and the subjective well-being gap between immigrants and natives, and various robustness checks. The main finding of this paper is that faltering perceptions of host country conditions are associated with less positive subjective well-being trajectories among a wide variety of first-generation immigrants in developed European countries and also to find that compared with natives, the more positive societal perceptions of first-generation immigrants are associated with a subjective well-being advantage. The findings provide useful suggestion for policy initiatives that seek to improve the subjective Well-being of immigrants and/or reduce the subjective well-being inequality between first-generation immigrants and natives. These insights also suggest that immigrants' perceptions of their conditions could play a role in determining their subjective well-being assimilation if these perceptions change

London International Conferences, 3-5 June 2021, hosted online by UKEY Consulting and Publishing, London, United Kingdom

over time. In particular, the findings suggest that a potential path towards more successful subjective well-being assimilation among immigrants would involve delaying or decelerating the process of immigrants'shifting frames of reference and faltering perceptions of host societies. While this paper concluded that one specific mechanism that is negatively related to subjective well-being assimilation, there may be other mechanisms that impair migrants' subjective well-being assimilation. This intervention could reduce immigrant frustrations about their perceived lack of progress in realizing their aspirations.

Rodriguez et al. (2019) 6 did the research entitled"Unaccompanied minors from the Northern Central American countries in the migrant stream"‖. The aim of this study is to examine whether variables such as age and the use of applications and social networks determine the personal learning environments (PLE) of unaccompanied foreign minors. The study provides insight into the differing circumstances leading to the current wave of childhood migrations from the northern countries of Central America. This paper focuses on unaccompanied migrant minors from the Global South to Europe and the United States. The researcher selected Descriptive, quantitative and cross-sectional research study. The ―PLE and Social Integration of UFMs‖ questionnaire was used as the study instrument. The sample of the present study was formed by 624 individuals (Male = 92.1%, Female = 7.9%) aged between 8 and 17 years old. The majority came from Morocco and resided in the cities of Ceuta and Melilla. The main findings of this paper were thousands of minors are migrating unaccompanied to high-income countries. The significant differences are highlighted in the personal learning environments as a function of age-related psychosocial factors as they pertain to unaccompanied foreign minors. Four factors were seen to exist in relation to the personal learning environments of unaccompanied foreign minors: self-concept of the learning process, planning and management of learning, use of resources and tools, and communication and social interaction. The same trend was observed in the four factors, with older age groups reporting better scores. The results show that the uses of applications and social networks have a significant and favourable impact on personal learning environment construction. As a result the finding suggest that frontline, street-level bureaucrats find themselves applying discretion wherever they can so as to protect their professional integrity and the wellbeing of children whose interests would otherwise be subjugated to the political expediency of the state and the for-profit contractors that the state hires. The study conclude that Germany's constitutional law, EU law, international law, and ethical principles each warrant the conclusion that greater investments in services to shelter and care for unaccompanied migrant youth are needed.

Thompson et al. (2019) 7 conducted a study on —Re conceptualizing agency in migrant children from Central America and Mexico‖. The study purpose is to explore the ways in which accompanied migrant children from Central America and Mexico express their agency despite limitations they may face as marginalized youth. In this study how these youth express their agency throughout the migration process as they confront authorities such as parents and immigration officers in their home countries, Mexico, and the United States. The researcher elected to apply thematic analysis and NVIVO qualitative analysis. The researcher draws from 32 in depth interviews and participatory activities between 13 and 18 years of age from Central America and Mexican children. It is found that migrant children from Central America and Mexico express this agency within socio – environmental contexts of the region that they originate from and more through. At present, these contexts include various threats from other agents and the environment. The study suggests that the observed negative impacts of agency suppression on participants' affect and behaviour suggest a need for further study from a behavioural science perspective. The study concludes thatbinary views of children's agency lead to an institutionalised suppression of children and young people. In light of growing number of child refugees and migrants in both Europe and America, it is urgent that the researcher gain a nuanced understanding of children's agency in order to developed efficient policies that both protect the best interest of the child and the state.

 Research gap identified on the basis of miscellaneous researches done on the topic of migration with respect to Migration of Agrarian Labour Force, Migration from Rural Areas of Bangladesh, Effects of Marital Status on Fertility of Rural-Urban and Urban-Rural Migrants, The Integration of Rural Migrants in New Settings, Migration and Income Differences between Black and White Men in the North, Working and Living Conditions of Migrant Workers in South America, Patterns of rural community Involvements, Migration of Hispanic Youth and Poverty Status, Information Gathcring, Prior Migration and the Land Factor in Family migration Decisions: Some Evidence from a Western Sub Sahara African Region, Continuity and Change in Rural Migration Patterns, etc. There are no notable investigations being done on the Muslim migrants of Tamil Nadu. And it is so a brand new to deal with *"Impact **of Migration on Personal Portrait of Migrants"***

6. Scope of The Study

The following are the scope of the study.

Geographical scope
This study covered the Muslim migrants from Tamil Nadu to Gulf Countries.

Topical scope
It focused on Muslim Migrants in the study area.

Time Scope
It Covered the Muslim Migrants to Gulf Countries during the period January 2014-January2019.

Analytical scope

The study analysed the significant change in the Personal Portrait of pre and post migration on migration in order to accomplish the objectives of the study.

Functional scope
It is to offer a set of meaningful suggestions to enhance the personal portrait of the migrants.

7. Objectives of the Study

The objectives of the study are given below:

- To analyse the Impact of Migration on Personal Portrait of Migrants.
- To suggest measures to enhance the Personal Portrait of the Migrants on Migration.

8. Research Methodology

a) Source

Both primary and secondary data was used for the study. The primary data was collected from the Indian Muslims who migrated from Tamil Nadu to Gulf countries. The major portion of the primary data was collected through an internet and referral survey. The secondary data was collected from annual records, guidelines, brochures and evaluation report maintained by Government of India and previous study.

b) Sampling Technique

Researchers have adopted the Snow ball non - probability sampling technique according to the availability of data.

c) Sample Size

The primary data was collected from **520** sample respondents by using structured questionnaire through SNSs (Social Networking Sites).

d) Study Area

The area of the study is limited to the Tamil Nadu Zone wise division namely North Zone which comprises of Chennai, Vellore, Kancheepuram,Thiruvallur, and Kallakurichi. South Zone includes Kanyakumari, Madurai, Ramanathapuram, Tirunelveli, and Tuticorin. East Zone includes Kodaikaanal, Natham, Nilakottai, Oddanchatram, and Palani. West Zone comprises of Coimbatore, Salem, Erode, Namakkal, and Dharmapuri.

e) Statistical Tools

The collected data were analyzed with the help of Paired't' test. The paired sample t-test, sometimes called the dependent sample t-test, is a statistical procedure used to determine whether the mean difference between two sets of observations is zero. In a paired sample t-test, each subject or entity is measured twice, resulting in pairs of observations. It might be to measure the performance of a sample of respondents before and after migration, and analyse the differences using a paired sample t-test using SPSS package.

9. Limitation of the Study

- It covers only migration of Muslims from India to Gulf countries.

- The data may not be free from the sampling errors and respondent's bias.

- This is the micro level study of Muslim migrants.

- The sample was restricted to 520 Muslim migrants.

- It is not possible to address many problems in a single research paper.

- This analysis does not include the Muslims who visit Mecca and Medina for pilgrimage purpose.

- The data was collected based on migrants from six Gulf countries which did not include Yemen because of its restless political scenario.

10. Hypothesis

The supposition for this analysis is based on whether the migrants face any remarkable or notable developments in their Personal Portrait. The following null hypotheses are tested as per Personal Portrait of before and after migration.

Null Hypothesis: H0: There is no significant change in the Personal Portrait of pre and post migration on migration.

Alternative Hypothesis: H1: There is a significant change in the Personal Portrait of pre and post migration on migration.

11. Impact of Migration on Personal Portrait: Analysis and Interpretation

The migrants' Personal Portrait of pre and post migration regarding Dressing Sense, Personal Grooming, Communication, Preference of Food, Eating Habit, Smartness, Habit of Smoking, Habit of Alcohol /Drug and Brand Preference are assessed. The responses of migrants about Personal Portrait before and after migration are tested with the help of paired 't' test. The $\bar{x}$, σ, 't' values and probability levels are given in Table -3.

London International Conferences, 3-5 June 2021, hosted online by UKEY Consulting and Publishing, London, United Kingdom

Table 3. Impact of Personal Portrait

Sl. No.	Factors	Mean $(\bar{x})$	Standard Deviation (σ)	Computed 't' Values at 5% level	Prob. level
1	Dressing Sense	0.297	0.457	14.05	0.00
2	Personal Grooming	0.641	0.480	26.50	0.00
3	Communication	0.186	0.459	8.87	0.00
4	Preference of Food	0.285	0.563	11.05	0.00
5	Eating Habit	0.170	0.449	8.16	0.00
6	Smartness	0.225	0.532	9.65	0.00
7	Habit of Smoking	0.032	0.176	3.80	0.00
8	Habit of Alcohol /Drug	0.023	0.295	1.63	0.00
9	Brand Preference	0.492	0.611	16.19	0.00

Source: Primary Data Collected from Sample Respondents

The difference between the scores of respondents before and after migration based on Personal Portrait is zero ($\mu=0$). On the basis of this assumption the following hypothesis is framed.

Null Hypothesis: H0: There is no significant change in the personal portrait of migrants before and after migration.

Alternative Hypothesis: H1: There is a significant change in the personal portrait of migrants before and after migration.

The result of the study revealed the followings:

The migrants' Personal Portrait of pre and post migration regarding Dressing Sense, Personal Grooming, Emotional Quotient, Brand Preference, Communication, Smartness, Eating Habit, Habit of Smoking, and Habit of Alcohol /Drug are assessed. The responses of migrants about Personal Portrait

before and after migration are tested with the help of paired'
test and 't' values are given in Table-3.

Dressing Sense: Majority of the migrants' were agreed that
their dressing sense and ability to choose clothes has been
improved after migration. i.e before migration they wear a
poorly designed, ill- fitting suit. After migration they know
how to dress in the most attractive way as possible. Now they
are wearing smart and stylish clothes. It is proved by "t" test
value 14.05.

Personal Grooming: The significant difference noted in
personal grooming (t=26.50, p=.000). Majority of the
migrants' were agreed that Personal Grooming is very much
improved due to migration and it is a universal truth. Before
migration personal appearance looking not good and the
migrants not focus on personal hygiene. After migration
migrants' posture can increase the masculine appeal and make
more sophisticated.

Emotional Quotient: t value 11.05 proved that migrants
Emotional Quotient enhanced between pre and post migration.
They enhanced their Emotional Quotient after struggling with
their emotions, cultural situation, and the medium used to
communicate. Before migration the migrants' are not able to
manage their emotions and Struggle to form strong
relationship. After migration the migrants' are able to control
impulsive feelings and behavior, manage the emotions in
healthy ways.

Brand Preference: Brand Preference creates funding or
approving investments to build, grow and protect. The
migrants improve their brand preference due to migration.
Before migration the migrants have low willingness to pay for
particular brands. After migration the majority of the migrants
typically buy a single brand, even when the alternatives are
objectively similar. It is proved by the t value 16.19.

Communication: The significance difference noted in Communication and proved by t=8.87. Before migration the migrants' struggle themselves in potential risks, associated with a crisis, where and how to inform stakeholders of their needs. But after migration it gives a better experience in education and employment opportunities, based on the construct of communication. They agreed that working place shape their communication better.

Smartness: Smartness is the quality of being intelligent. Due to migration the migrants, had great maturity and smartness and they able to think quickly in different situation. Before migration the migrants have no dedication in boost the brain power. But after migration the migrants' are practicing certain lifestyles habit to improve overall intelligence. The result t value =9.65 shows the positive impact on post migration.

Eating Habit: Eating habit also shows the positive change between pre and post migration. Before migration the migrants follow poor meal planning, Skipping breakfast and eat unhealthy food. But after migration the migrants take care of the body through a healthy diet, nutritious food, exercise routine and become health conscious to stay safe and return safe to home land. The statement is supported by the t value 8.16.

Habit of Smoking, Alcohol /Drug: Habit of Smoking and Alcohol /Drug also show positive change between pre and post migration. Migrants' poverty, lack of education and unemployment influence the abuse of these habits. But, mild changes only observed after migration and the migrants have the addiction and they feel positive and feel good as habit and it is proved by t value for habit of smoking is 3.80 and habit of alcohol/drugs is 1.63 respectively.

12. Findings

London International Conferences, 3-5 June 2021, hosted online by UKEY Consulting and Publishing, London, United Kingdom

The following shows the major findings arrived from the analysis.

- The study identified that the notable changes in migrants' Personal Grooming, Communication, Preference of Food, Eating Habit and Smartness.

- The result revealed that migrants looked their unhealthy behaviour such as smoking, consuming of alcohol and drugs as habits.

- t' Test proved that there is a significant change in the Personal Portraits of pre and post migration

13. Suggestions

Through these analysis the following suggestions are made

- The migrants should strengthen the positive impact on self portrait to heal self.

- They should wane their unhealthy behaviour to become role model for the potential migrants of homeland

14. Conclusion

It is concluded from the study that the notable changes have been identified in migrants' Personal Grooming, Communication, Preference of Food, Eating Habit and Smartness. Besides, the result revealed that migrants' looked their unhealthy behaviour such as smoking, consuming of alcohol and drugs as habits. The migrants should strengthen the positive impact on self portrait to heal self and become the best human capital for the home land and the country they live...Besides, they should wane their unhealthy behaviour to become role model for the potential migrants of homeland.

15. Scope for Further Exploration

- Migration of people before and after COVID 19

- Impact of migration on the personal portraits of migrants can be extended based on the parameter such as the geographical area, sample size, topic, analysis and time.

- Innovative research on alternative measures to safeguard the migrants abroad.

- Any Institution or organization led by the migrants for enhancing employability in their homeland.

- Analysing the chances that hinder migration or improve migration in the coming years.

Note:

The primary data collected from 520 sample respondents by Dr. A. Ayisha during her Ph.D Research work. She pursued her research work under Dr. R. Malini and she was awarded Ph.D degree on 06.01.2021. This present paper based on the data collected by using structured Questionnaire via SNSs for the research work entitled "Causes and Consequences in the Migration of Indian Muslim to Gulf Countries-A Study with Special Reference to Tamil Nadu"

References

Kumari, S. (2014), ―Rural-urban migration in India: Determinants and factors. International Academy of Science‖, Engineering and Technology, Vol. 3, No 2, pp 161–180.

Chandrasekhar, S. & Sharma, A.(2015), ―Urbanization and spatial patterns of internal migration in India‖, Spatial Demography, Vol. 3, No 2, pp 63-89. URL; http://www. igidr.ac.in/ pdf /publication/WP-2014-016.pdf.

Sasi, A. & Santha, S. (2017), ―Migrant labourers in Perumbavoor‖, International Journal of Management, IT & Engineering, Vol. 7, No 2, pp 21-33.

Ali, I., CP, Abdul Jaleel & Bhagat, R. B. (2017), ―Level and gender differentials in inter-state out-migration in India‖, Border Crossing Vol. 7, No 1, pp 13-34.

Hendriks, M., Burger, M., & De Vroome, T. (2018), ―Unsuccessful subjective wellbeing assimilation among immigrants: The role of shifting reference points and faltering perceptions of the host society‖, Journal of Immigrant and Refugee Studies, Vol.17, No 3, pp 279-298.

Rodriguez, Nestor, Ximena Urrutia-Rojas, and Luis Raul Gonzalez. (2019), ―Unaccompanied Minors from the Northern Central American Countries in the Migrant Stream: Social Differentials and Institutional Contexts‖, Journal of Ethnic and Migration Studies Vol. 45, No 2,pp 218–234.

Thompson, Amy, Rebecca MariaTorres, Kate Swanson, Sarah A. Blue and Óscar Misael Hernández Hernández. (2019), ―Re-conceptualising Agency in Migrant Children from Central America and Mexico‖, Journal of

London International Conferences, 3-5 June 2021, hosted online by UKEY Consulting and Publishing, London, United Kingdom

Ethnic and Migration Studies, Vol.45, No 2, pp 235–
252.

https://www.toppr.com
http://www.arabnews.com
https://shodhganga.inflibnet.ac.in
https://www.statisticssolutions.com/
https://www.skillsyouneed.com

London International Conferences

londonic.uk

ukeyconsultingpublishing.co.uk

Kyrgyz and its Challenges for Language Processing

Yahya Polat
yahya.polat@iaau.edu.kg

Alimjan Zakirov

Abstract

We present a short survey and exposition of some of the important aspects of Kyrgyz that have proven challenging for natural language processing. Most of the challenges stem from the complex morphology of Kyrgyz and how morphology interacts with syntax. We also provide a short overview of the major tools and resources developed for Kyrgyz natural language processing if there is any so far.

Keywords: Kyrgyz, Morphology, Syntax, NLP

London International Conferences, 3-5 June 2021, hosted online by UKEY Consulting and Publishing, London, United Kingdom

How Fair is Education Policy in Albania?

Albana Cekrezi
Epoka University
acekrezi17@epoka.edu.al

Abstract

Democracy, although a highly debated concept, preserves its identity in the values upon which it is founded. These values give universality to democracy, are normative and define democracy. Fairness is considered as one of the standard values of democracy. It is seen as justice, social justice and as equality. Fairness is highly discussed from the prospect of distributive justice. As injustice comes from unfair distribution of resources, the criteria over which this distribution is done is important. Three are the main principles based on which fair distribution is conducted: equality; everyone receives the same resource; equity, resource is distributed based on merit, work, talent; need, resource is distributed based on what individuals need. The development of political culture is the bridge that links fairness with citizens. Education stands as an important tool that influences political culture. At the same time, it is one

London International Conferences, 3-5 June 2021, hosted online by UKEY Consulting and Publishing, London, United Kingdom

of the spheres where to notice issues of fairness. In education, a top-down analysis of fairness necessitates the examination of education policy. The driving research question has been to examine how education policy in Albania reflects issues of fairness. It brings results from the analysis of formal documents representing education policy. Content analysis has been used as a method aiming to filter these documents for issues related to fairness.

Keywords: democracy, education, fairness, education policy

London International Conferences, 3-5 June 2021, hosted online by UKEY Consulting and Publishing, London, United Kingdom

1. Introduction

Democracy has been the subject of debate since its genesis in ancient Greece. Mainly, its political and *democratic culture development* aspects are among the discussed categories, even to these days (Kurki, 2010). Recently, the shift of deliberation has moved towards the values democracy promotes. *Values* are pondered over many models of democracy because they reduce the disputation over which democracy has been internationally contested as a concept. Secondly, these values overcome the lack of universality which characterizes many models of democracy as typifying national contexts. Furthermore, values are normative and they uncover the obscure and non-ideal aspects of democracy (Kuyper, 2016). Lastly, values and their embodiment best characterize democracy (White, 1999). The civic virtues of citizens among others define the quality of democracy (Almond & Verba, 1989) (Putnam, 2000). Nowadays, values are part of the civic competence framework next to attitudes, knowledge, and skills (Council of Europe, 2018); (Hoskins, Villalba, & Van Nijlen, 2008). Democratic values represent the 3rd face of democracy, next to popular sovereignty, rights and liberties, and economic democracy (Sodaro M. J., 2004).

Democracy consists of a constellation of key values and *fairness* is among the most important ones. It is considered as one of the standards along with freedom (Munck, 2014) and can be traced to many models of democracy. Justice (Aristotle & Jowett, 1999) guided the Athenian citizenry, even though it was restricted to Athenian adult males (Held, 2006). Fairness characterized democracy in the city-republics with equality of men before God, self-determination, and accountability of the political community only to itself (Held, 2006, p. 34). Laws were to be made by all people (Tierney, 2014) and citizens were encouraged to be *equally* represented in a mixed form of government (Balot & Trochimchuk, 2012). Equality was assured and regulated through the general will, the agreement among the citizenry and government, in Rousseau`s Social Contract (Wade, 1976). Locke`s understanding of the state of nature was related to the *freedom and equality* of reasonable individuals (Lucci, 2018). Similarly, Mill advocated for equality between genders (Ten, 1969).

2. Fairness

Fairness is one of the main values upon which democracy is constructed. When arguing on fairness, it is inevitable not to mention justice or equality. Fairness, social justice, or simply justice are used to refer to similar ideas. They cover various domains in the political, social and economic life. Social justice is viewed as part of human rights education (Vienna Declaration and Programme of Action , 1993). Justice is connected strongly to reasonableness which consists of some reasonable conditions on which to make a choice, be acceptable and have support (Mandle, 1999).

Nevertheless, the idea of fairness rests in the fair distribution of resources. The *distribution of goods* is at the heart of justice (Reidy, 2010). This distribution is the essence of justice. *Distributive justice* deals with the distribution of goods or resources and concerns three actors: the distributor, the distributed and the observer (Jasso, Törnblom, & Sabbagh, 2016). From Rawls's point of view, distributive justice has to do with income equality and unequal distribution should be applied only to the benefit of the least advantaged ones. The distributed goods are not solely limited to financial goods but include other resources as well such as: positions, influence, knowledge, etc. Miller (1992, p. 559) notes that there are three main criteria to be considered about justice "*desert, equality and need*". These criteria define the way how goods are being distributed and represent the conditions or standards over which decisions are made. The understanding of fairness is guided by these three components. The distribution of goods is based on these criteria. As a result, their abandonment leads to injustice. For instance, the criteria of equity (desert) stresses effort, work and talent (Rawls, 1971, 1999, p. 32). Equality refers to sameness and need of equal distribution of what individuals necessitate. In education, the just distribution is based on these detailed values or norms: *equality* means offering equal opportunities to all; *need*, offering opportunity based on what the individual, in this case, students need (Resh & Sabbagh, 2016, p. 350); *equity*, offering opportunities according to individual characteristics, like someone`s ability, effort, performance or work (Konow & Schwettmann, 2016).

Rawls describes justice as an important value with two principles (Bentley, 1973). The first principle deals with the equality of rights/ liberties and duties. The second principle offers inequalities in two cases:1. Inequality related to positions, based on equality of opportunity to all, and 2. (the difference principle) offers economic and social inequalities (income to active members of the society) only to compensate for the least advantaged individuals. Rawls` ideas resonate with the ones mentioned above. In terms of inequalities, they can be applied only to fulfil the principle of need and merit. Offering economic or social support to the citizens in need fulfills the criteria of need. Similarly, offering inequalities to individuals based on their capabilities reverberates with the principle of merit. This is to provide some equality of opportunity. Equality of opportunity includes equal chances given to all in terms of education and culture; open positions and the arrangement of institutions (operating within the context of free market). Additionally, equal opportunities for students despite their class differences (Rawls, 1971, 1999, p. 63). For this principle, he uses two conditions: (1) a just or fair institution (2) the individual that has *"taken advantage of the opportunities it offers to further one's interest"* (Rawls, 1971, 1999, p. 96). Rawls does not directly mention equality of educational opportunities, but he only states that it is a means in achieving wealth, status, and other social goods (Klees & Strike, 1976) and the state should do more than just provide education of high quality for the least advantaged (Wenar, 2008, 2017). The first steps for the principles of justice deal with the requirements and rules of justice (Rawls, 1971, 1999, pp. 171-176). For this, the achievement of fairness passes through just or fair institutions and the rules or regulations they follow.

3. Fairness in Policy Documents

In democracies, democratic values are part of the political culture (Duch & Gibson, 1992). Political culture includes norms that are accepted widely. In democracies, political cultures consist of democratic values (Duch & Gibson, 1992). Political culture never remains static, but changes over time. It is dependent on the source of the values that furnish it and the process through which these values are formed. The source of values gains importance and education, among others, is one of them. The quality of political development is related to the quality of education next to the economy and urbanization (Cutright, 1963). Naturally, the education of a country reflects some sets of values (Hahn, 1999). Schools and education are considered social institutions (Selznick & Steinberg, 1969). These social units may influence one's understanding of politics (Almond & Verba, 1989, pp. 266-267).

From a top-down perspective, the quest for fairness starts with the examination of education policy. Education policy has to do with context, text and implementation (Taylor, Rivzi, Lingard, & Miriam, 1997). In terms of context, the education policy in Albania is oriented towards international and European programs like *European Union's Education Benchmarks for 2020 and SDG4-Education 2030* (UNESCO; IZHA, 2017). The content of education policy is found in the *texts* or *documents* that represent it. For this reason, we aim to explore fairness as presented and understood through the perspective of education policy documents. Thus, the following research question is posed:

<u>R.Q.</u> How is fairness addressed in education policy documents as concerns their hierarchy of importance, the types used to represent these values through the direct and indirect forms and the outlook policy documents have of these values?

   1. *What is the hierarchy of importance for these values as found in policy documents?*

   2. *What aspects(types) of fairness are found in policy documents?*

   3. *Are these aspects referred to directly or indirectly?*

   4. *What understanding of fairness do these documents have?*

4. Methodology

In order to answer this research questions, it was seen appropriate using content analysis as a research methodology. Content analysis is a method of inquiry that uses texts or images, symbols etc. to make inferences (Krippendorff, 2004, p. 18). Although content analysis is typically used in a quantitative manner, it can be approached in a less strict manner when including qualitative nuances (Cardno, 2018, p. 633). In such research, Kracauer (1952-1953) suggests more than one-sided quantitative analysis. Qualitative analysis is found in the logical organization of categories, in connections among them, in the interpretation, explanation, analysis and quest for the significance of the results. In content analysis, inferences on the text can help to give answers to research questions (White & Marsh, 2006). Inferences can be made on the significance of the presence or absences of certain entities.

In content analysis the following steps were utilized: *unitizing, sampling, coding, representation, inferring, giving results*

(Krippendorff, 2004, p. 84). *Unitizing* in this case has to do with the identification of key terms that are central and of interest for this research. In this case they are related to fairness. The direct and inferred terms of this values have been detected from the examination of the theory and literature review. *Sampling* refers to the limitation of the documents to be evaluated. Here, the researcher made use of relevance sampling which refers to the *intentional selection of the possible texts* or documents that serve the purpose of the inquiry. As a result, the documents have been restricted to those dealing with education policy in Albania. Policy document analysis as a method of research has some advantages. Many of these documents are easy to find and reach; they can be managed easily and attained at a low cost. Even though, depending on the nature of policy document, some of them may be difficult to find or they may contain unsatisfactory information.

Four key official documents representing education policy were selected: The Law on Pre-university Education, the Strategy of the Pre-university Education 2014-2020 (Eurydice, 2019), the Curricular Frame and The Curricular Manual for Social Sciences. To begin with, the Law on Pre-University Education enjoys the highest position in rank regarding the legislation on education. The Strategy of the Pre-university Education for 2014-2020 sets out lines on how to develop national education policy. Normally, *strategy* is used to define the way to reach the aims that have been highlighted by policy (UNESCO, 2013). The Curricular Frame is the essential curriculum document which outlines aims, competences, and results expected from students in relation to their skills, attitudes and knowledge (On Pre-University Education System in the Republic of Albania, 2012). It sets in broad lines all what the curricula is about: formal documents, applied curricula and perceived curricula (The Curricula Framework of the Pre-University Education of the Republic of Albania, 2014,

p. 22). The Curricular Frame is part of the curricula documents. It was included in this part in order to be analyzed together with other policy documents because it is the *main* document that mirrors the policies and strategies of development in education (The Curricula Framework of the Pre-University Education of the Republic of Albania, 2014). Curricula only reflects in content the above-mentioned documents. The Curricular Manual for Social Sciences is part of the documents of the curricula and includes standards to be achieved by students in social sciences and lines of themes included in subjects (IZHA, 2010). It is a detailed reflection of the Curricular Frame.

After this phase, the researcher tried to apply computer *coding* through NVivo. Computer coding refers to the usage of software to code words, analyze themes and texts. The usage of computer software and the development of a code list allows for reliability and transparency (DeBell, 2013). In this case, NVivo uses qualitative resources such as text, documents, visuals; analyses them based on pre-determined themes; visualizes them through charts, maps etc. (https://www.qsrinternational.com/nvivo-qualitative-data-analysis-software/home, 2020). Finally, it offers possibility for interpretation of the findings. Before applying computer coding, the researcher developed a coding list. The coding list for this chapter was generated after scanning carefully the literature on fairness. Initially, there were identified the main *direct* and *inferred terms* for the values of fairness. The theory pointed to the key general terms, like the types of fairness. In case there was reference to key words like: fairness, unfairness, justice, equality, need, merit etc. the categorization was *direct terms*. On the other hand, if there was reference to justice based on equality, equity or need indirectly, they were categorized under indirect terms. A list with *key words* related to fairness found from the literature is presented in the table below.

London International Conferences, 3-5 June 2021, hosted online by UKEY
Consulting and Publishing, London, United Kingdom

Table 1. List of key words related to fairness

Fairness	
Direct Terms	**Indirect Terms**
Fairness	**General**
Justice,	reasonableness
social justice,	transparency
global justice,	lack of bias
distributive justice	impartiality and consistency
Equality,	just rules, regulations, procedure, structure,
political equality,	opportunity, aims, means, society,
social equality,	treatment
equality of policies,	independent criterion
equal say,	retribution, punishment, apology
equal voice,	restoration of relation
equality of votes,	**Equity**
equality in access,	opportunities based on individual
equality in	characteristics, ability, effort, performance,
membership,	work, sacrifices, contribution, meritocracy
participation,	**Equality**
equal education,	same opportunities
equality of	educational inequality
opportunity,	diminish the differences
equal chances,	*educational achievement inequality*
equality of rights/	same quality of education
liberties and duties	decentralization
desert,	access to information and means
merit,	inclusiveness, *inclusive practices*
equity,	**Need**
need,	disadvantaged family, background, social
opportunity based	class, less/ least advantaged, family income
on need	aspects of injustice,
	schools in deprived areas, different
	economic, social and cultural backgrounds
	individualism, exclusion, ICT
	violence, hatred, nationalism, corruption,
	favoritism

After this phase, the selected policy documents were scanned to see if there were other key terms of reference to be added to the code list. The codification of the policy documents was thematic. This enabled the researcher to critically explore the documents according to the main themes of fairness, their subtypes and the way they were represented by the policy documents. During this process, if the researcher noted different forms of reference from what was detected before from the literature, she added them to the initial list and the result was a more comprehensive list of key terms. So, codification in policy documents has been done based on themes following the list with the key words. During the codification, the researcher found also some terms that were indirectly related to fairness. Eventually, 7 codes were used in NVivo, as presented below under fairness.

Table 2. List of Codes used for fairness in NVivo

Fairness Themes	
Fairness Direct	Fairness Indirect
Fairness Direct Equality	Fairness Indirect Equality
Fairness Direct Need	Fairness Indirect Equity
	Fairness Indirect Need

5. Results

Figure 1. Hierarchy of Fairness

The hierarchy above demonstrates that fairness in the indirect version occupies more space than the direct version. The indirect form is found coding issues on equality, need and lastly equity.

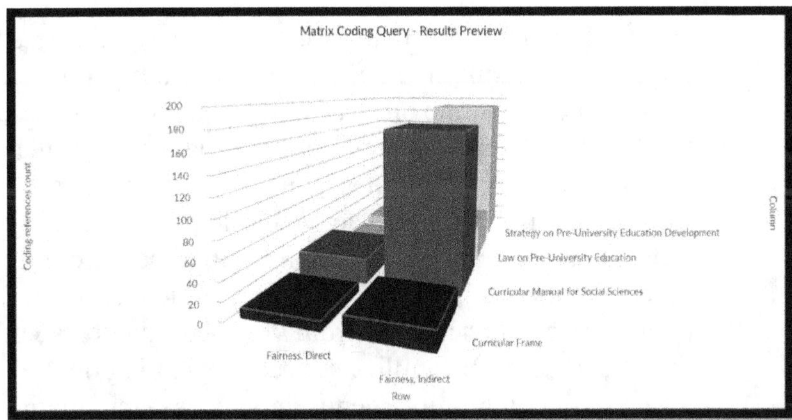

Figure 2. Matrix coding query-Fairness Direct-Indirect relation

In this matrix we observe that the value of fairness is coded mostly in an indirect form compared to the direct version. The documents where it is mostly found are: the curricular manual for social scienced and the strategy on pre-university development.

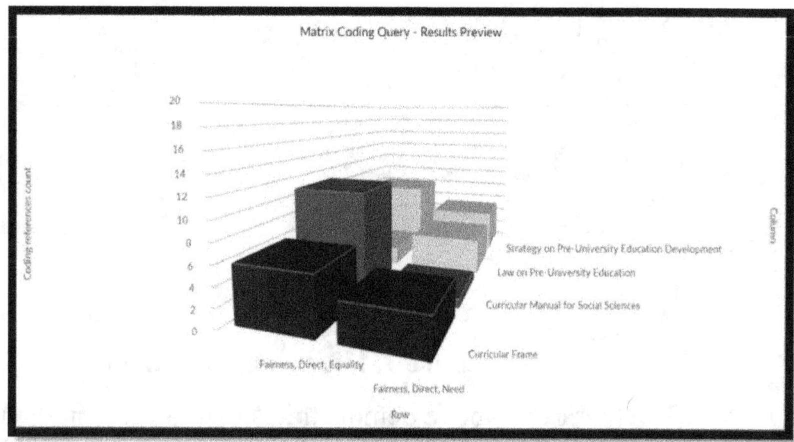

Figure 3. Fairness direct form coded as equality and need.

We notice that forms that have been coded as fairness based on equity are missing. Fairness based on equality, direct version is found to concentrate on issues like: equality, equal education for all, equal opportunities, gender equality, curricula that enables equal opportunities, equal protection, equality of understanding, equal and active participation, equality in education etc. Fairness based on need, direct reference addresses issues like: the curricula have to respond to needs, adapting the curricula according to needs, students with special needs, students of families in need, depending on the needs of the school community, identifying needs, accreditation of programs based on needs etc.

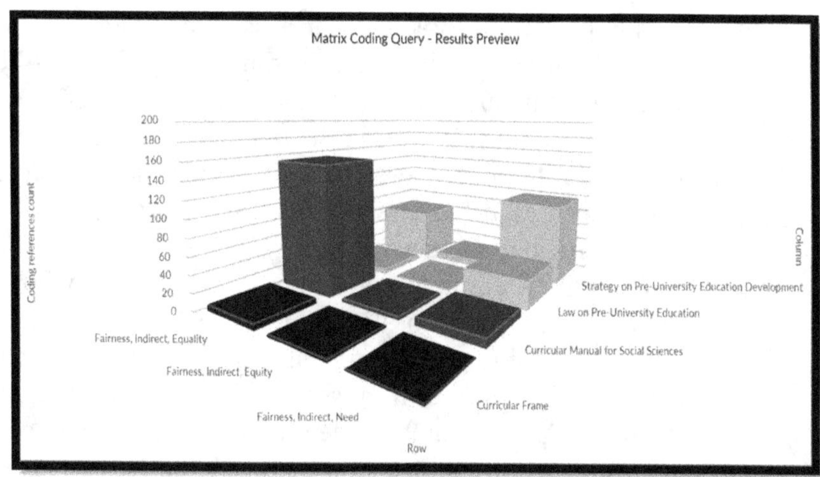

Figure 4. Fairness indirect version

Fairness in the indirect version has been coded from the policy documents as addressing equality, equity and need. Most of the codes relate to fairness as based on equality, followed by need and less by equity. This is inclusive for all the 4 education policy documents. This may be interpreted as: fairness is mostly understood as equality in education policy documents. A more detailed explanation is given below.

Fairness has been coded more as based on equality, indirect form. Education policy documents address issues related to lack of fairness and equality indirectly such as marginalization, discrimination or poverty in general. Policy documents address issues such as: each person has the right to education, each student can be successful, learning chances for all, each student should be given the chance to demonstrate himself. Additionally, it should be mentioned that topics related to law, respect for law, breaking the law, the aim of the law and constitution are common as well.

It is important to show that fairness is not solely given in the light of equality. Fairness, according to education policy documents includes a wide range of cases that represent need and equity. For instance, in the light of fairness based on need (indirect reference) there are cases coded such as: protection for minorities, differentiated tasks, respect for the developmental characteristic of students, the usage of a variety of assessment forms, disabled students, students with learning difficulties, support for disabled, institution of special education, home schooling , education in prison, psycho-social service, education for minorities, education for the children of the migrants, scholarship, meeting the educational needs of the community, refunding school texts, lack of infrastructure etc. , Al these point to awareness of needs.

Fairness based on equity is found only in the indirect version. Some of the references addressing equity are: depending on the availability of students; possibility for extra courses; differentiated tasks[1], project; according to the interest of students; refinement of knowledge based on students` interest; appropriate assessment of students; based on performance; scholarship; successful students etc.

6. Discussion

The development of political culture is the bridge that links fairness with citizens. Education stands as an important tool that influences political culture. At the same time, it is one of the spheres where to notice issues of fairness. In education, a top-down analysis of fairness necessitates the examination of education policy and education policy documents are the starting point of this examination.

---

[1] This has been coded both for need and equity as it may be a course addressing needs, or a course for further refinement of knowledge addressing equity.

London International Conferences, 3-5 June 2021, hosted online by UKEY Consulting and Publishing, London, United Kingdom

Education policy documents in Albania reflect fairness from the perspective of equality, equity and need. Fairness as equality is understood in the equality between genders, equality in opportunities, equality in education, and in equal rights for students. Fairness from the specter of need, addresses issues related to protection of individuals, students in need, focus on students with learning difficulties, with disabilities, education for special groups (minority, migrants) and importance of infrastructure. Fairness understood as equity is found in the emphasis of the interest of students, reward given based on performance, stimulation through scholarship and promotion of successful students.

Education policy documents recognize students in need, recognize merit and talent. However, mostly, fairness is equalized to equality. It occupies more space with references such as: each person has the right to education, each student can be successful, learning chances for all etc. Fairness based on equity has only been addressed indirectly. Even though, education policy covers the three main criteria of distributive justice, these findings need to be investigated further in order to examine how policy is applied in schools.

London International Conferences, 3-5 June 2021, hosted online by UKEY Consulting and Publishing, London, United Kingdom

References

Almond, G. A., & Verba, S. (1989). *The Civic Culture-Political Attitudes and Democracy in Five Nations.* Newbury Park, California: Sage Publications, Inc.

Aristotle, & Jowett, B. (1999). *Politics.* Kitchener: Ont: Batoche Books.

Balot, R., & Trochimchuk, S. (2012). The Many and the Few: On Machiavelli's "Democratic Moment". *The Review of Politics, 74*(4), 559-588.

Bentley, D. J. (1973). A Theory of Justice. *University of Pennsylvania Law Review, 121*(5), 1070-1078.

Cardno, C. (2018). Policy Document Analysis: A Practical Educational Leadership Tool and a Qualitative Research Method. *Educational Administration: Theory and Practice, 24*(4), 623-640.

Council of Europe. (2018, April). *Reference Framework of Competences for Democratic Culture.* Retrieved from Council of Europe: https://www.coe.int/en/web/campaign-free-to-speak-safe-to-learn/reference-framework-of-competences-for-democratic-culture

Cutright, P. (1963). National Political Development: Measurement and Analysis. *American Sociological Review, 28*(2), 253-264.

DeBell, M. (2013). Harder Than It Looks: Coding Political Knowledge on the ANES. *Political Analysis, 21*(4), 393-406. Retrieved from https://www.jstor.org/stable/24572671

Duch, R. M., & Gibson, J. L. (1992). "Putting Up With" Fascists in Western Europe: A Comparative, Cross-Level Analysis of Political Tolerance. *The Western Political Quarterly, 45*(1), 237-273.

Eurydice. (2019, 28 March). *Legislation and Official Policy Documents-Albania.* Retrieved from Eurydice: https://eacea.ec.europa.eu/national-policies/eurydice/content/legislation_en

Hahn, C. L. (1999). Citizenship Education: An Empirical Study of Policy, Practices and Outcomes. *Oxford Review of Education, 25*(1/2), 231-250.

London International Conferences, 3-5 June 2021, hosted online by UKEY Consulting and Publishing, London, United Kingdom

Held, D. (2006). *Models of Democracy*. Cambridge and Malden: Polity Press.

Hoskins, B., Villalba, E., & Van Nijlen, D. (2008). *Measuring Civic Competence in Europe-A Composite Indicator based on IEA Civic Education Study*. Luxembourg: Institute for the Protection and Security of the Citizen, Centre for Research on Lifelong Learning (CRELL).

https://www.qsrinternational.com/nvivo-qualitative-data-analysis-software/home. (2020, March). Retrieved from https://www.qsrinternational.com: https://www.qsrinternational.com/nvivo-qualitative-data-analysis-software/home

IZHA. (2010). *Curricular Frame-Social Sciences*. Retrieved from ascap.edu.al: https://ascap.edu.al/Biblioteka/6Udhezues%20te%20Pergjith shem/Shkencat-Shoqerore-Shkenca-Shoqerore.pdf

Jasso, G., Törnblom, K. Y., & Sabbagh, C. (2016). Distributive Justice. In C. Sabbagh, & M. Schmitt, *Handbook of Social Justice Theory and Research* (pp. 201-218). New York, Heidelberg, Dordrecht, London: Springer.

Klees, S. J., & Strike, K. A. (1976). Justice as Fairness: Coleman's Review Essay on Rawls. *American Journal of Sociology, 82*(1), 193-201.

Konow, J., & Schwettmann, L. (2016). The Economics of Justice. In C. Sabbagh, & M. Schmitt, *Handbook of Social Justice Theory and Research* (pp. 83-106). New York, Heidelberg, Dordrecht, London: Springer.

Kracauer, S. (1952-1953). The Challenge of Qualitative Content Analysis. *The Public Opinion Quarterly, 16*(4), 631-642.

Krippendorff, K. (2004). *Content Analysis-An Introduction to its Methodology*. Thousand Oaks, London, New Delhi: Sage Publications.

Kurki, M. (2010). Democracy and Conceptual Contestability: Reconsidering Conceptions of Democracy in Democracy Promotion. *International Studies Review, 12*(3), 362-386.

Kuyper, J. (2016). *Global Democracy-The Stanford Encyclopedia of Philosophy*. Stanford : Metaphysics Research Lab, Stanford University.

Lucci, D. (2018). Political Scepticism, Moral Scepticism, and the Scope and Limits of Toleration in John Locke. In *Yearbook of the Maimonides Centre for Advanced Studies* (pp. 109-143). De Gruyter.

Mandle, J. (1999). The Reasonable in Justice as Fairness. *Canadian Journal of Philosophy, 29*(1), 75-107.

Miller, D. (1992). Distributive Justice: What the People Think. *Ethics, 102*(3), 555-593.

Munck, G. L. (2014). What is Democracy? A Reconceptualization of the Quality of Democracy. *Democratization, 23*(1), 1-26.

On Pre-University Education System in the Republic of Albania. (2012). *Law nr.69/2012 On Pre-University Education System in the Republic of Albania*. Tirana, Albania.

Putnam, R. D. (2000). *Bowling Alone-The Collapse and Revival of American Community*. New York: Simon and Schuster.

Rawls, J. (1971, 1999). *A Theory of Justice- Revised Edition*. Massachusetts: Harvard University Press.

Reidy, D. A. (2010). Rawls's Religion and Justice as Fairness. *History of Political Thought, 31*(2), 309-343.

Resh, N., & Sabbagh, C. (2016). Justice and Education. In C. Sabbagh, & M. Schmitt, *Handbook of Social Justice Theory and Research* (pp. 349-367). New York, Heidelberg, Dordrecht, London: Springer.

Selznick, G. J., & Steinberg, S. (1969). *The Tenacity of Prejudice: Anti-semitism in Contemporary America*. New York: Harper and Row.

Sodaro, M. J. (2004). *Comparative Politics-A Global Intruduction- Second Edition*. New York: McGraw-Hill.

Taylor, S., Rivzi, F., Lingard, B., & Miriam, H. (1997). *Educational Policy and the Politics of Change*. London and New York: Routledge.

Ten, C. L. (1969). Mill and Liberty. *Journal of the History of Ideas, 30*(1), 47-68.

The Curricula Framework of the Pre-University Education of the Republic of Albania. (2014). Retrieved from https://ascap.edu.al/: https://ascap.edu.al/wp-content/uploads/2017/03/Korniza-Kurrikulare.pdf

Tierney, B. (2014). Marsilius of Padua. In B. Tierney, *Liberty and Law* (pp. 122-141). Washington, D.C: Catholic University of America Press.

UNESCO. (2013). *UNESCO Handbook on Education Policy Analysis and Programming-Education Policy Analysis.* Bankok: UNESCO.

UNESCO; IZHA. (2017). *Albania-The Analysis of Education Policy-Issues and Recommendation.* Paris: UNESCO.

Vienna Declaration and Programme of Action . (1993, June 25). Retrieved from OHCHR: https://www.ohchr.org/Documents/ProfessionalInterest/vienna.pdf

Wade, I. O. (1976). Rousseau and Democracy. *The French Review, 49*(6), 926-937.

Wenar, L. (2008, 2017, January 9). John Rawls. In E. N. Zalta, *The Stanford Encyclopedia of Philosophy.* Stanford, California, U.S.A: Metaphysics Research Lab, Stanford University. Retrieved from Stanford Encyclopedia of Philosophy: https://plato.stanford.edu/entries/rawls/#TwoGuiIdeJusFai

White, M. D., & Marsh, E. (2006). Content Analysis: A Flexible Methodology. *Library Trends, 55*(1), 22–45.

White, P. (1999). Political Education in the Early Years: The Place of Civic Virtues. *Oxford Review of Education, 25*(1/2), 59-70.

Improving Teachers' Professionalism Through Blended-Based Training in Indonesia's Remote Area

Albert Efendi Pohan

Riau Island University, Batam City, Riau Island Province, Indonesia

albert.efendipohan@gmail.com

Hilman Mudawali Daulay

Senior High School 1 Barumun Tengah, North Sumatra Province, Indonesia

hilmanmudawalidly@gmail.com

Agus Sahrir

Vocational High School 5 Batam City, Riau Island Province, Indonesia

sahrir@smkn5batam.sch.id

Abstract

Blended-based training is a best alternative choice for equalization of training in Indonesia's district area in the Covid-19 pandemic era considering the low competency of teachers in Indonesia at this time. This research was applied on improving the teachers' professionalism in Indonesia's remote area in order to act their main roles on preparing the learning administration. The research method used was experimental research by one-group pre-test and post-test design. Research

London International Conferences, 3-5 June 2021, hosted online by UKEY Consulting and Publishing, London, United Kingdom

subject were from normative and adaptive teacher at in remote areas of North Sumatera Province in Indonesia with 31 teachers. The instrument which used was portfolio and individual test by writing the lesson plan and all tasks collected by google drive. The data analysis technique was performed using SPSS Statistic 20 by one simple paired t-test. The result of this study showed that blended-based training could improve the teachers' profesionalism where the significan value (2-tailed) was 0.00 < 0.05. It mean that there was a significant difference of values where the post-test score was bigger than the pre-test score.

Keywords: Blended-Based Training, Professionalism, Remote Area

1. Background

It has been approved in the global agreement that teachers have very important roles in education because they have tasks to developing collaborative learning plans (Gutierez, 2020), developing competencies, potential and student skills (Stemberger, 2020), and measuring the results of student learning progress (De Simone, 2020). For this reason, teachers are required to have high professionalism to carry out their duties professionally. According to Abusowman and Osaigbovo (2020) the professional skills of teachers involve the methods, strategies and techniques used in the teaching process which include effective classroom management, motivating skills, teaching methods, evaluation strategies, preparation of learning plans and the use of teaching materials effectively. Furthermore, Olohundare (2020) states that professional teachers must be more dedicated to their work regularly by preparing their lesson administration, entering the classroom at the right time, ensuring that students have a better understanding of the material being taught, taking detailed notes on the development of students and pay attention to difficulties that prevent students from learning effectively. In the other hand, professional teachers must be able to manage the class well because they can create supportive conditions for directing and regulating student social behavior (Omenka and Otor, 2015).

Previous empirical studies have shown that teacher competence in Indonesia really needs to be improved (Siswandari, 2013; Lestari and Purwanti, 2018; Rohmat, 2019). This is because the teacher is one of the determinants of the success of education (Dwirahayu, et al, 2020) and also as an external factor (Dahar 2011; Syarifuddin, 2011) which affected the implementation of education system, beside the factors from within students and factors in mastery of subject matter (Dahar, 2011). In addition, teachers need to understand the material to transfer knowledge, teachers also need to master competence in the field of research, mastery of curriculum, development of teaching materials, lifelong learning, socio-cultural competence, emotional competence, communication skills, mastery of education technology, mastery of the environment (Selvi, 2010; Olga, 2012, Dwirahayu, et al. 2020), mastery of class management, mastery of assessment methods, and problem solving skills (Peklaj, 2015). But the facts in the field showed that in general the competence of teachers was still low and has not been able to carry out the ideal view above (Maulipaksi, 2016; Yuliana, 2020) this was indicated by a low teacher competency testing score of 5.7 nationally (Minister of education and culture of Indonesia, 2020).

Yuliana (2019) revealed that the actual problem of teachers was related to learning devices which made formally to fulfill administrative needs alone, there were many teachers who were unable to compile a syllabus of learning devices independently, and teachers who compiled learning devices were not based on competencies that would be achieved. This problem was caused by teacher training in Indonesia that has not been carried out evenly and sustainably, especially in Indonesia's outermost, underdeveloped and remote areas due to geographical conditions (Lantip, et al 2017). The implementation of training was not carried out based on the evaluation results of previous trainings. The trainings were only focused in several provincial capitals and other large cities. However, the central government does not prioritize disadvantaged areas, so the professional level of teachers is very low. In general, teachers in remote areas did not understand the changing systems and objectives of the curriculum in Indonesia. However, the central government has never taken this problem seriously and until now the central government has not provided a solution to overcome this big problem.

The problems above were in line with the results of the interview with the principal of the senior high school in remote areas on March 14, 2021. The information from 45 adaptive and normative teachers have never been included in training to increase teacher professionalism related to the policy of independent learning. They did not understand the concept of the latest curriculum established by the ministry of national education in Indonesia. They were still used the old curriculum and were unable to follow the target of the national curriculum. This condition occurred because the central government could not reach the school location which very far from the central government.

The actual problems above were the main reason for researchers to conduct this research to improve teacher professionalism through blended training in senior high school in remote areas of north Sumatra province in Indonesia. This training model was chosen because of the conditions of Covid-19 which forced all countries to work to find solutions so that the education process could be held (Rahayu and Wirza, 2020). Another reason was due to the strict implementation of lockdowns including educational institutions both in Indonesia and in other countries (Syauqi, Munandi, and Triyono, 2020; Napitupulu, 2020). Blended-based training is a training which is carried out online using the help of platforms and face-to-face training. Blended training was a training activity which combines face-to-face learning activities using internet media (Hidayat et al., 2020; Ahmad et al., 2020; Ningsih et al., 2017). Blended training could increase self-regulated participants and in the end could increase the final result effectively and efficiently (Usman, 2019). This was in line with research conducted by Abdullah (2018) stated blended training model could increase effectiveness in learning and training.

The results of research conducted by Saovapa Whicadee (2017) showed that blended training was an effective way to achieve better results because it could increase abilities through active participation in online classroom communities. This research also showed that blended training could improve content connectivity and interactivity among teachers in various modes of learning opportunities. With the use of technology support, the course would provide more collective knowledge and web-based applications on assignments outside of training that would benefit participants.

Furthermore, research conducted by Agus Subaidi et al (2019) showed that blended training could increase teacher professionalism. This was because implementation could help teachers in the training process apply in the learning process. Training provided flexibility where training could be carried out even if it was not face to face. Subsequent research conducted by Sudjana et al (2019) showed that blended training could increase learning effectiveness, expanded learning reach, time and cost efficiency and improved final outcomes.

According to Nana Sujana (2000) professionalism is a skill that people have according to their profession. This is in line with Sadirman (1993) who states that professionalism is the ability to do something that is owned by certain people. Furthermore, Ahmadi (1992) defines professionalism as a job characterized by shrewdness or intellectuality. Meanwhile, teacher professionalism is the teacher's ability to actualize himself in doing his job in everyday life (Ibrahim Bafadal, 2000). Based on the theoretical building above, it can be concluded that teacher professionalism is the ability of teachers to carry out their main duties as a teaching staff which includes activities to make learning preparations, the learning process and learning evaluation.

Professional teachers have characteristics which appear in carrying out their duties at school. According to Sadirman (1993) the characteristics of a professional teacher were: a) able to identify deficiencies, weaknesses, difficulties, and problems that exist within him. b) establish a program to increase the ability of teachers to overcome deficiencies, weaknesses, difficulties. c) formulate the objectives of the learning program. d) determine and arrange learning materials and media. e) determine the format and prepare the assessment tool. f) create and schedule learning activities. g) assess learning outcomes. h) follow up in the form of remedials and enrichment for students based on the results of objective assessments.

The professionalism of teachers in their profession as teaching staff according to Hadi Supeno (1995) were; a) mastering learning materials according to the subjects they are teaching, b) managing learning activities, managing classes, c) using various media and relevant learning resources, d) understanding the principles of education, e) managing the activities of the learning process, f) providing an assessment of student learning outcomes, g) understanding the functions and guidance programs, h) mentoring and counseling, i) understanding and preparing school administration, j) and understanding the principles and interpret research results. In addition to having professional abilities, teachers must also have a professional attitude such as being willing to do additional assignments, showing patient behavior and being able to adapt to the school environment, having a constructive, responsible and collaborative attitude, always developing themselves, and a spirit of teaching students.

Based on the explanation above, it can be formulated the formulation of the problem of this research is whether mixed-based training can improve teacher professionalism in Indonesia's remote areas north Sumatra province?

2. Research Methodology
The research method used was experimental research. According to Sugiyono (2019) the experimental research

method is a quantitative method used to determine the effect of the independent variable (treatment) on the dependent variable (result) under controlled conditions. While the type of experimental research applied in the field was the One-group pretest-posttest design. This type of research was conducted by one group of subjects by giving a pre-test followed by giving treatment and given a post-test to determine the effect of the treatment by comparing the pre-test and post-test values. An overview of this type of research can be seen in the chart below.

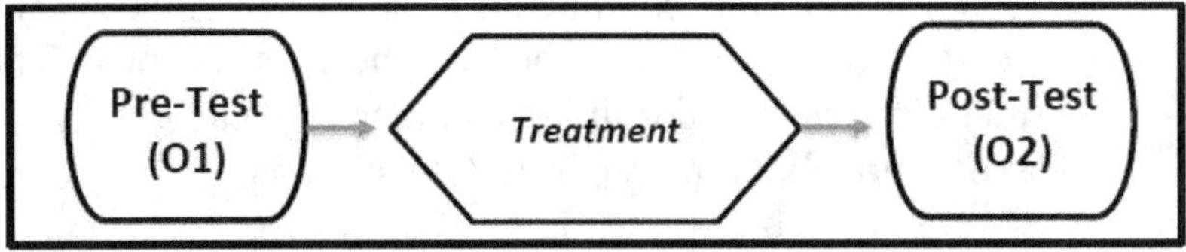

Figure 1. Type of *One-group pretest-posttest design* Sugiyono (2019)

This research was conducted in Indonesia's remote area north Sumatra province in academic year 2020-2021. This research was conducted by cooperation with the education office of the province of North Sumatra of the Gunung Tua branch of district Padang Lawas Utara. Mixed-based training was held in the laboratory of SMA Negeri 1 recently using the zoom meeting platform and having the discussion with the team. This school is located at Jalan Kh. Dewantara number 15, Barumun Tengah District, Padang Lawas Regency North Sumatera Indonesia. The subjects of this study were 31 teachers who were normative and adaptive both civil servants and government contract teachers. The first data collection technique to be used as a pre-test value before being given treatment was through a portfolio by assessing the lesson plan which arranged by the teachers before giving the blended training. Furthermore, the researcher provided blended-based training, namely online and face-to-face training for 4 meetings through the zoom meeting platform for online and 4 meeting for group discussion and doing project of training. The Next, the researcher collected the second data to be used as a post-test score by assessing the lesson plan which arranged by the teachers after giving the blended training. The results of this assignment are carefully assessed using a previously developed rubric. The data collecting of this study were processed by using statistical applications to determine the results of the normality test and hypothesis testing and to present the results in tables and graphs. The data analysis of this research was explained if the post-test value (O2) > the pre-test value (O1) then the hypothesis is accepted. This means that blended-based training can increase teacher professionalism in preparing lesson plans.

3. Result And Discussion
3.1. Findings

The results of this study were obtained through an assessment of the lesson plan which developed by 31 teachers in Indonesia's remote area north Sumatra province in academic year 2020-2021 before giving treatment and after giving treatment. The following results of the research are presented in table below.

Table 1. Result of Pre-Test dan Post-Test

Indikacors	Result	
	Pre-Test	Post-Test
Total value	1956	2430
Averge score	63.10	78.39
Highest score	78	90
Lowest score	50	55
Median	64	80
Modus	64	80

Table 1 above shows the teacher's ability to arrange the lesson plan where the mean score of the teacher in the pre-test is

63.10 and the post-test is 78.39. The table above also illustrates the profile of the teacher's ability in preparing a lesson plan where the lowest teacher score in the pre-test is 50 and the post-test is 55. Furthermore, the highest score in the pre-test is 78 and 90 post-test. Those who are declared competent in arranging the lesson plan are to obtain a minimum score of 70. Below is a diagram of the percentage of the teacher's ability in arranging the lesson plan.

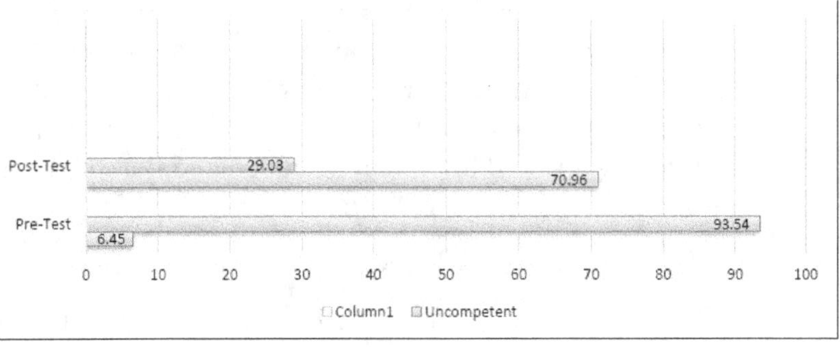

Figure 2. The Comparison of Pre-Test and Post-Test

3.2.   Normality Testing

The normality test was carried out by using SPSS analysis using the One-Sample Kolmogorov-Simirnov Test. The decision making in this test is if the significance value (Sig.) was bigger than 0.05, the research data was normally distributed. Meanwhile, if the significance value (Sig.) was smaller than 0.05, the research data was not normally distributed. Below are the results of the One-Sample Kolmogorov-Simirnov Test for normality.

Table 2. The Result of One-Sample Kolmogorov-Simirnov Test

		Unstandardized Residual
N		31
Normal Parameters[a,b]	Mean	0E-7
	Std. Deviation	4.72991779
Most Extreme Differences	Absolute	.110
	Positive	.110
	Negative	-.074
Kolmogorov-Smirnov Z		.611
Asymp. Sig. (2-tailed)		.849

Based on table 2 above, it can be seen that the results of the normality test with the One-Sample Kolmogorov-Simirnov test can be described as normal. This shows that the significance value is $0.849 > 0.05$, it can be concluded that the residual value is normally distributed.

3.3. Hypothesis Testing

This hypothesis test used the Paired Simple t-test to determine whether the application of blende-based training could improve teacher professionalism in Indonesia's remote area of North Sumatera Province. The basic of decision making was if the significance value (2-tailed) < 0.05 then there was a significant difference between the pre-test and post-test scores. And if the significance value (2-tailed) > 0.05 then there was no significant difference between the pre-test and post-test scores. Below are the results of the hypothesis test.

Tabel 3. The Result of Hypothesis Testing by Paired Simple t-test

		Paired Differences					t	df	Sig. (2-tailed)
		Mean	Std. Deviation	Std. Error Mean	Lower	Upper			
Pair 1	Variabel O1 - Variabel O2	-15.290	5.001	.898	-17.125	-13.456	-17.022	30	.000

Based on the results of the hypothesis test in table 3 above, it can be seen that there is a significant difference between the pre-test and post-test scores of teachers in remote areas of North Sumatera Province in Indonesia after participating in blended training. This is indicated by the results of the Paired Simple t-test where the significance value (2-tailed) is 0.00 < 0.05. In accordance with the basis for the conclusion above, it can be concluded that blended training has given the effect on improving teachers' professionalism in remote areas of North Sumatera Province in Indonesia in the academic year 2020-2021.

3.4. Discussion

This study aimed to measure the effect of blended training through experimental research. The results of the hypothesis test showed that the blended training could improve the professionalism of teachers in remote areas of North Sumatera Province in Indonesia. Professionalism referred to in this case was the ability of the teacher to prepare the lesson plan in accordance with the provisions of independent learning. The ability to arrange learning administration was a characteristic of professional teachers (Gutierez, 2020) and then applied it to improve student competence (Stemberger, 2020), and measured the results of student learning progress (De Simone, 2020). There were several reasons blended training could increase the professionalism of teachers in remote areas of North Sumatera Province in Indonesia such as collaboration among the teachers, flexibility of training time, face-to-face online communication and enthusiasm of training participants.

Based on the statement of the principle of senior high school in remote areas of North Sumatera Province in Indonesia, the teachers have never attended this training, especially in the Covid-19 conditions. This condition made all school activities carried out from their respective homes so that teacher collaboration was not well-established to hold discussions and share experiences as usual. By this blended training, teachers could collaborate actively where they could learn more effectively and efficiently from one another. This is in line with Saovapa Wichadee (2017). By this training teachers could effectively develop a newest model learning implementation plan through digital collaboration which consists of developing learning objectives to be achieved, developing learning activities, and assessing learning outcomes (Minister of education and culture of Indonesia, 2019).

This blended training model has flexibility where teachers could attend the training from their respective homes and face to face through the zoom meeting application. This training model could assist teachers in the learning process in an applicable way in the learning process. This training provided flexibility where training could be carried out even though it was not face-to-face, but participants could follow it well (Agus Subaidi et all, 2019). Teachers could learn the training materials after completing the training held by rewatching the available recordings. Teachers also could deepen the training material anytime effectively and efficiently. This was in line with Sudjana et al (2019) where mixed-based training could increase learning effectiveness, expanded learning reach, time and cost efficiency and improved final outcomes.

 Blended training was very helpful for teachers to master the training materials because through this mode teachers easily established the communication to solve problems and difficulties to do the working. Teachers have the opportunity to communicate effectively both in online classrooms and outside

Albert E. Pohan
Hilman M. Daulay
Agus Sahrir

online classrooms. This was in line with Tubagus et al (2019) which stated that blended training of trainees has the opportunity to develop communication skills both in class and outside the classroom through online interactions with each other discussing common problems and could optimize learning in improving individual learning. Through this training teachers could work together to complete training assignments effectively. In general, the making of a one-sheet learning implementation plan for teachers at remote area in North Sumatra Indonesia was still new because they have never had the opportunity to take part in training. However, through this training they could learn individually and collaboratively to compile the lesson plans that they will apply in the teaching process.

Indeed, blended training could create new conditions that have never been experienced by teachers as training participants. So that this condition affected the level of enthusiasm of the trainees. Blended training not only provided a learning experience, but also provided a quality and friendly learning environment as a whole. This was in line with research results conducted by (Wai and Seng, 2014; Tubagus et al, 2019). For this reason, blended training was the most appropriate choice in the Covid-19 pandemic season to increase the training effectiveness, efficiency and greater attractiveness in interacting with people in a diverse learning environment. This mode offered the opportunity to study together separately and at the same time and at different times, so that the Covid-19 pandemic does not become an obstacle to learning.

This blended training was a solution to the unequal problem of teacher training in Indonesia. Previously, teachers who had to attend training to improve professionalism had to leave the workplace because they had to attend training in the provincial capital and generally went to the capital city of Indonesia. From the information that the authors found in the field that the cost of this blended-based training was cheaper than the previous direct training costs. Previous training held by the central government had very high costs, such as hotel fees, transportation for trainees, lodging and consumption costs. However, in this blended training, the costs mentioned above were completely unnecessary because participants could attend the training from their own homes or from their respective schools. Blende-based training provided a very large opportunity to provide training to teachers in disadvantaged areas. Thus the problems of unequal training in Indonesia could be overcome. So that the priority of increasing the teachers' professionalism could be carried out to improve the quality of Indonesian education, both in big city centers and in many remote areas in Indonesia.

4. Conclusion and Recommendation
4.1. Conclusion

Based on the above discussion, the results of this study can be concluded that the blended training conducted by researchers could increase the teachers' professionalism in Indonesia's remote area North Sumatra, especially the competence of arranging the lesson plan. Where the results of hypothesis testing with paired simple t-test showed that the significance value (2-tailed) was $0.00 < 0.05$. It means that there was a significant difference in values where the post-test score was bigger than the pre-test score.

4.2. Recommendation

Based on the research conclusions above, the authors can provide suggestions to researchers, teachers, and school principals in order to:

1) Implementing blended training to improve teachers' professionalism in arranging the lesson plan, especially in the current Covid-19 pandemic era.

2) Conducting similar research with different or the same variables to improve teachers' professionalism in arranging the lesson plan, carrying out teaching, and conducting learning assessments.

3) Conducting the same research with different variables in other remote areas in Indonesia to improve teachers' professionalism in arranging the lesson plan, implementing teaching, and conducting learning assessments.

4) Providing equitable training based blended training to the teachers in the others remote areas, underdeveloped and outermost in Indonesia to improve teachers' professionalism in arranging the lesson plan, implementing teaching, and conducting learning assessments.

5) Follow up on the results and realization of training in outermost, underdeveloped and remote areas schools in Indonesia to ensure the effectiveness of learning process.

References

Abdullah, W. (2018). *Blended Learning Model in Increasing Learning Effectiveness.* Fikrotuna, 7(1), 855–866. https://doi.org/10.32806/jf.v7i1.3169

Achmadi. (1992). *Islam as a Paradigm in Educational Sciences.* Semarang: Aditya Media, hlm. 271. 24

Agus Subaidi, Moh Zayyadi, Hasanah. I. S, dan Durroh Halim. (2017). Blended Learning Training for Teachers in the Environment of Madrasah Tsanawiyah Negeri Sumber Bungur. *JPM (Journal of Community Empowerment) ISSN : 25411977 E- ISSN : 25411977 Vol.4 No. 2 2019.*

Ahmad, Perwira Negara, H. R., Ibrahim, M., & Etmy, D. (2020). Online Learning Training (Google Classroom) For Teachers of MTs dan MI Nurul Yaqin Kelanjur. JPMB : Journal of Character Community Empowerment, *3(1), 66–79.* *https://doi.org/10.36765/jpmb.v3i1.224*

Dahar, R.W. (2011). *Learning and Teaching Theories.* Jakarta: Erlangga Publisher.

Dwirahayu, G., Satriawati, G., Afidah., & Hafiz, M. (2020). Analysis Of Mathematics Teachers' Pedagogical Competency In Madrasah Tsanawiyah (Mts) In Developing Scientific-Based Lesson Plan. *Jurnal Pendidikan dan Kebudayaan, Vol. 5, Nomor 1, Juni 2020.* DOI : 10.24832/jpnk.v5i1.1551.

Hadi Supeno. (1995). *Profile of Teacher.* Jakarta: Pustaka Sinar Harapan Publisher.

Hidayat.M.T, Teuku Junaidi, Effendi. D.I. (202). Blended Learning training Through Mobile Platform For Junior High School Teacher in Covid-19 Pandemic. *International Journal of Community Service Learning. Volume 4 Nomor 3 2020, pp 200-208 E-ISSN: 2549-6417 P-ISSN: 2579 -7166 DOI: DOI: http://dx.doi.org/10.23887/ijcsl.v4i3.29094*

Ibrahim Bafadal. (2000). *Improving of Teachers' Professionalism.* Jakarta: PT. Bumi Aksara Publisher.

J.J. De Simone. (2020). The Roles of Collaborative Professional Development, Self-Efficacy, and Positive Affect in Encouraging Educator Data Use to Aid Student Learning, Teacher Development. *An International Journal of Teachers' Professional Development.* DOI: 10.1080/13664530.2020.1780302.

K.A. Omenka dan E.E. Otor. (2015). Influence of Classroom Management on Students' Academic Achievement in Science and Mathematics in Oju Local Government Area of Benue State. *Global Journal of Interdisciplinary Social Science, vol. 4, no. 4, pp. 36-40, 2015. [Online] Available:*

Lantip, D.P., Wibowo, U.D., & Arum, D.H. (2017). Curriculum Management Of Teacher Professional Program For Frontier, Outermost, And Least Developed Regions In Universitas Negeri Yogyakarta. *Jurnal Pendidikan dan Kebudayaan, Vol. 2, Nomor 1, Juni 2017.*

Lestari, Y.A. & Purwanti, M. (2018). Relationship of Pedagogic, Professional, Social, and Teachers' Personality Competencies in Non-formal School. *Educational Journal, 2(1),197-208.*

Lia Yuliana. (2019). Achievement Of National Education Standards In Senior Secondary Schools. *Jurnal Pendidikan dan Kebudayaan, Vol. 4, Nomor 2, Desember 2019.* DOI : 10.24832/jpnk.v4i2.1457

Maulipaksi, D. (2016). Seven Provinces for Teacher Competency Test 2015. https://s.id/wP3Nw accessed on Sunday, 03 January 2021 at 3.30 WIB

Napitupulu, Rodame Monitorir. (2020). The Impact of the Covid-19 Pandemic on Distance Learning Satisfaction. *Jurnal Inovasi Teknologi Pendidikan* 7(1): 23–33.

Ningsih, Y. L., Misdalina, M., & Marhamah, M. (2017). Improvement of Learning Outcomes and Learning Independence of Statistical Methods through Blended Learning. Al-Jabar: *Jurnal Pendidikan Matematika, 8 (2), 155. https://doi.org/10.24042/ajpm.v8i2.1633*

Olga N. (2012). The Competencies of the Modern Teacher. Paper presented at the Annual Meeting of the Bulgarian Comparative Education Society (10th, Kyustendil, Bulgaria, Jun 12-15, 2012). https://files.eric.ed.gov/fulltext/ED567059.pdf.

Peklaj, C. (2015). Teacher Competencies Through the Prism of Educational Research. *Center for Educational Policy Studies Journal, 5(3), 183-204.*

Regulation of the Ministry of Education and Culture of the Republic of Indonesia Number 22 of 2020 concerning the Strategic Plan of the Ministry of Education and Culture

Rahayu, Retno Puji, and Yanty Wirza. (2020). Teachers' Perception of Online Learning during Pandemic Covid-19. *Jurnal Penelitian Pendidikan* 20: 392–406.

Rohmat Sulistiya. (2019). Heutagogy As A Training Approach For Teachers In The Era Of Industrial Revolution 4.0. *Jurnal Pendidikan dan Kebudayaan, Vol. 4, Nomor 2, Desember 2019. DOI: 10.24832/jpnk.v4i2.1222*

Sally B. Gutierez. (2020). Collaborative Lesson Planning as a Positive 'Dissonance' to the Teachers' Individual Planning Practices: Characterizing the Features Through Reflections-On-Action, Teacher Development. *An International Journal of Teachers' Professional Development. DOI: 10.1080/13664530.2020.1856177.*

Saovapa Wichadee. (2017). A Development of the Blended Learning Model Using Edmodo for Maximizing Students' Oral Proficiency and Motivation. *International Journal of Emerging Technologies in Learning. Vol. 12. No. 02 (2017). https://doi.org/10.3991/ijet.v12i02.6324.*

Sardiman, A. M. (1993). *Teaching and Learning Interaction and Motivation.* Jakarta: CV. Rajawali Publisher, hlm. 28.

Selvi, K. (2010). Teachers' Competencies. Cultura. *International Journal of Philosophy of Culture and Axiology, 7(1),167-175.*

Siswandari dan Susilaningsih. (2013). The Impact of Teacher Certification on the Improvement of the Learning Quality of Students. *Jurnal Pendidikan dan Kebudayaan, 19(4), 487-498.*

Sugiyono, Sugiyono. (2019). *Quantitative Approach Management Research Methods, Qualitative, Combination (Mixed Method), Action Research , and Evaluation Research.* In *Book Chapter,* ed. Setiyawan. Bandung: Alfabeta Publisher.

Sujana, I.M., Waluyo, U., Soepriyanti, H., dan Arifuddin. 2019. Google Classroom (GC) Based Blended Learning Development Workshop as a Classroom Action Research and Learning Solution. Journal of Education and Community Service. 2. (1)

Sulyman Kamaldeen Olohundare. (2020). Assessment of Teachers' Dedication, Discipline, Knowledge and Skills in Kwara State Basic Schools, Nigeria. *Journal of Education and Learning (EduLearn) Vol. 14, No. 4, November 2020, pp. 537-542 ISSN: 2089-9823 DOI: 10.11591/edulearn.v14i4.16524*

Sunday Bello Abusomwan dan Louis Osaigbovo. (2020). Competency Improvement Needs of Teachers of Brick/Block Laying and Concreting Works. *Journal of Education and Learning (EduLearn) Vol. 14, No. 4, November 2020, pp. 517-524 ISSN: 2089-9823 DOI: 10.11591/edulearn.v14i4.16450.*

Syarifuddin, A. (2011). Application of Learning Cooperative Learning Model and the Factors which Influenced . Ta'dib: *Journal of Islamic Education (Jurnal Pendidikan Islam), 16(01),   113-136.* http://jurnal.radenfatah.ac.id/index.php/tadib/article/view/57.

Syauqi, Khusni, Sudji Munadi, and Mochamad Bruri Triyono. (2020). Students' Perceptions toward Vocational Education on Online Learning during the COVID-19 Pandemic. *International Journal of Evaluation and Research in Education 9(4): 881–86.*

Tina Stemberger. (2020). The Teacher Career Cycle and Initial Motivation: The Case of Slovenian Secondary School Teachers, Teacher Development. *An International Journal of Teachers' Professional Development.* 24:5, 709-726, DOI: 10.1080/13664530.2020.1829023.

Tubagus,M., Muslim,S. & Suriani. (2019). The Impact of the Development of Blended Learning Models Using Computer Applications In Higher Education. *International Journal of Educational Research Review, 4(4), 573-581.*

Usman, U. (2019). Blended Learning Based Educational Communication in Establishing Independent Learning. *Jurnal Jurnalisa, 4 (1), 136–150.* *https://doi.org/10.24252/jurnalisa.v4i1.5626.*

Wai, C. C., & Seng, E. L. K. (2014). Exploring the Effectiveness and Efficiency of Blended Learning Tools in a School of Business. *Procedia-Social and Behavioral Sciences, 123, 470-476.*

The State of Education and Artificial Intelligence After the Pandemic

Ibrahim Eren Bisen
Rice University
Ebisen2003@gmail.com

Fatih Nalcaci
Texas A&M
Fatihschool2@gmail

Sriram Alagappan
University of Texas
sriram.alagappan@utexas.edu

Yetkin Yildirim
Rice University
yetkin@rice.edu

Abstract

The neologism of artificial intelligence and machine learning brought a myriad of conveniences and advantages into the education sector. These new and improved technologies have the potential to be the remedies to the predicaments that have emerged from the rapid transition into online learning and the problems that have existed with traditional learning. These predicaments vary from personalized learning experiences, administrative busy works, to increased overall student interaction. This article explores how artificial intelligence became the new normal in education and the recently revealed benefits of artificial intelligence and machine learning in

London International Conferences, 3-5 June 2021, hosted online by UKEY Consulting and Publishing, London, United Kingdom

Ibrahim Eren Bisen
Fatih Nalcaci
Sriram Alagappan
Yetkin Yildirim

developing automated solutions to these predicaments such as Intelligent Tutoring Systems (ITS), dynamic schedules, automated grading, and increased personalized student interaction through chat-bots. Along with these solutions, some of the economical advancements that these technologies will bring include new research and investments in AI development, data collection and understanding, and increased jobs. These advancements are on a massive scale and will need to be addressed. By accommodating our resources into the advancements in this area we can make our education more versatile, engaging, and inclusive.

Keywords: education, artificial intelligence, machine learning, intelligent tutoring systems (ITS), Chat-bots, dynamic schedules, automated grading, I-it and I-thou, educational data, learning management systems (LMS), emergency online learning, remote learning, personalized learning

London International Conferences, 3-5 June 2021, hosted online by UKEY Consulting and Publishing, London, United Kingdom

Ibrahim Eren Bisen
Fatih Nalcaci
Sriram Alagappan
Yetkin Yildirim

1. Introduction

The COVID-19 pandemic has been the cause of many drastic changes around the world in the past year, and one of the sectors most affected by these changes was education. Students were quickly transferred from face-to-face to online instruction and have had to adapt to new styles of testing, attendance, interaction, and assignments. As a result, many students have spent significant amounts of time interacting with computers and technologies. Artificial intelligence, which will be referred to as AI for the remainder of this article, is one of these technologies that has attempted to maintain and support the educational infrastructure during this time. Furthermore, this increasing reliance on technology has caused AI to become integrated in almost all of the educational applications, from learning management systems to chat-bots. With online learning becoming the new normal and AI having an increased role in this reality, it is important to analyze the current systems in place and the educational and economic contributions it brings.

2. AI and machine learning in education

Before delving into the potential of AI in education, it is important to develop a basic and fundamental understanding of AI and machine learning. However, because it is such an interdisciplinary field, definitions range from a multitude of disciplines such as neuroscience, psychology, economics, mathematics, linguistics, biology, and more. For one to be able to describe AI within the education sector, they must first rely on a concept within AI called machine learning (Luckin R. et al., 2016). Machine learning refers to the way certain computer programs and algorithms can learn from given data and analyze and learn the patterns within the given data. For this paper, AI will be described as "[The automation of] activities

Ibrahim Eren Bisen
Fatih Nalcaci
Sriram Alagappan
Yetkin Yildirim

that we associate with human thinking, activities, such as decision-making, problem-solving, learning …" (Bellman, 1978). This idea centers around creating a computer system that can learn and make rational decisions independently, and thus mimic human intelligence and reasoning.

The handwritten digit recognition problem is a classic case of machine learning which can help describe these concepts. This problem has an important role in automating the process of reading handwritten documents such as bank checks. A machine learning algorithm's first job is to learn to read. This can be done by feeding the algorithm a dataset. For example, the United States National Institute of Science and Technology (NIST) has a database of digits that can be used to train and test an algorithm (Grother P. J., 1995). These algorithms will typically use a form of a neural network, a computer system of virtual nodes which simulates neurons in a brain, to read and classify the digits based on their pixel values. Certain features like the location of the pixels, number of loops, etc. are identified by the algorithm, which is then used to make a guess. Weight values in the nodes of the neural network are adjusted based on whether this guess was correct or not, thus allowing the algorithm to learn and improve as it reads more digits. An example of an error rate recorded by a machine learning algorithm in the handwritten digit problem is 0.56%. As a comparison, humans are estimated to have an error rate ranging from 0.2% to 2.5%.

London International Conferences, 3-5 June 2021, hosted online by UKEY
Consulting and Publishing, London, United Kingdom

Ibrahim Eren Bisen
Fatih Nalcaci
Sriram Alagappan
Yetkin Yildirim

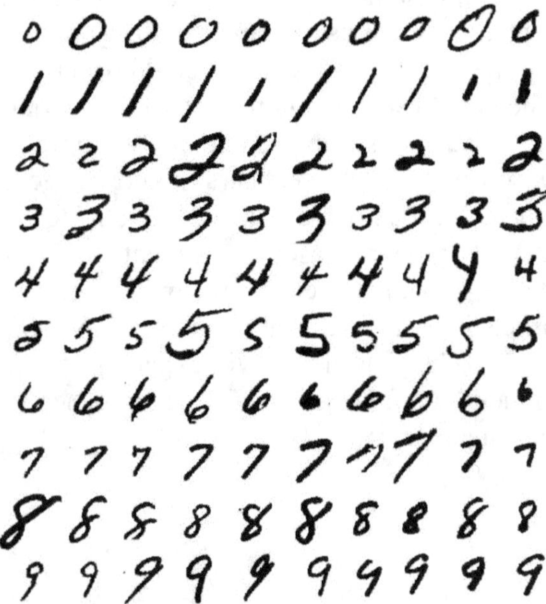

Figure 1. NIST Handwritten Digits (Grother P. J., 1995)

2.1 Benefits of AI

Artificial intelligence (AI) has already made a profound impact across various industries, but the events of COVID-19 have helped propel its influence even further, especially in the education sector. A recent report from 2020 shows that AI investments in education totaled $295.4 million — still far less than investments made in AI in industries like banking, retail, healthcare, and telecommunication, which averaged more than $2 billion each. (Soohoo S., 2020). However, the forced migration of education from in-person to online as a result of COVID-19 created an unprecedented demand for automated educational systems. As a result, students gained a more personalized learning experience as deadlines became more

Ibrahim Eren Bisen
Fatih Nalcaci
Sriram Alagappan
Yetkin Yildirim

relaxed, problems allowed for more trial and error, grading became more fair as human error and judgment was removed from the system, and learning could occur at the student's pace as they could search and revisit class material at any time. More advanced systems could analyze graded material like quizzes in order to detect certain knowledge gaps of a student (Lynch, 2020). Coursera, an educational tech company, is an example of the increased investment and growth in this industry in the past year, as the public company opened to the markets in early 2021 with a market cap of $5.9 billion USD (León 2021). This article will expand upon specific AI systems and their benefits that have helped to generate this increased investment.

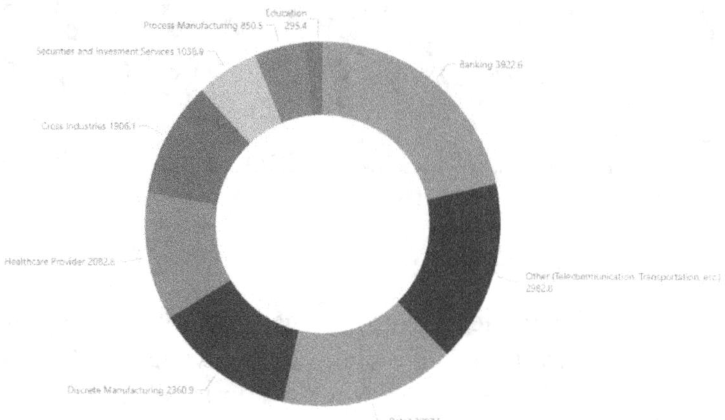

Figure 2. Worldwide Cognitive / AI Spending by industry.
(Soohoo S., 2020)

2.2 Personalized learning

One advantage of using AI in education is its potential to personalize learning. With the help of AI, class curriculum can be uniquely modeled and distributed to each student based on

Ibrahim Eren Bisen
Fatih Nalcaci
Sriram Alagappan
Yetkin Yildirim

their strengths and weaknesses, making the learning process more efficient and flexible. Moreover, students can quickly skim through material they are already familiar with, allowing them to spend more time focusing on new or challenging material. Thus, rather than having to follow the class, each student can learn at their own pace. This revolution of increased individualism in education is a message conveyed by the Organization for Economic Co-operation and Development (OECD) in order to improve the industry, and AI is a fundamental tool to help reach this goal (Lynch, 2020).

2.3 Intelligent tutoring systems

An Intelligent Tutoring System (ITS) is a type of modern AI tool that helps to achieve the goal of personalized education. An ITS helps students learn by providing step-by-step tutorials that guide them through their course content. The ITS is able to adapt its teaching method to individual student needs by creating a understanding of the student's general grasp of the material. It is also responsive to the student by analyzing the student's performance and providing guidance and feedback when necessary (Holmes et al. 2019). One of the challenges of an ITS is that it must determine when to provide guidance and how much guidance to provide, as giving no help or too much help can impact how much the student learns.

There are three primary approaches to ITS: the domain model, the pedagogical model, and the learner model. The domain model is the simplest of the three, as it only contains knowledge of the learning material. As a result, there is no personalization in this approach as the system can only provide learning material based on what it knows. The pedagogical model expands on this model by acquiring personal data about the student, allowing it to provide hints and tips to the student while learning. It can also determine what and when the student needs to review certain concepts. The learner model

Ibrahim Eren Bisen
Fatih Nalcaci
Sriram Alagappan
Yetkin Yildirim

tracks the students' performance, adjusting curriculum and lessons based on properties like grades and emotional states (Holmes et al. 2019). This type of ITS is built off neural networks, allowing them to improve at providing a better learning experience by identifying patterns in the student's learning ability, something that would be hard, if not impossible, for humans to identify. As a result, ITS helps simulate a one-on-one tutoring experience, an effective teaching method that is not feasible in an in-person classroom environment.

2.4 Exploratory learning environment

Exploratory Learning Environments (ELE) are another application of AI in education. ELEs function by providing the student with hands-on experiences that teach broader concepts rather than just telling and describing it, and uses artificial intelligence to . While this method is less structured, it provides a more student participation in the teaching method (Holmes et al. 2018). Overall, ELEs trade some control and structure in their teaching process for a more self-centered, interactive learning experience.

2.5 Chatbots

While ITS and ELE's focus on the content delivery of the knowledge, AI chatbots assist with the interactive classroom elements. Virtual assistants have risen to prominence in other industries via phone systems and websites that offer basic customer support, and these technologies have recently garnered interest in education as well. For example, The Common App, a college admissions website, provides a chatbot named Oli which guides students through the admissions process (Sandoval 2018). Resources like this have helped significantly during the pandemic, when students lack access to in-person college admissions guidance. Chatbots can also assist students by providing them with administrative

Ibrahim Eren Bisen
Fatih Nalcaci
Sriram Alagappan
Yetkin Yildirim

guidance in a class such as test details, due dates, grades, etc. (Sandoval 2018).

2.6 Administrative benefits

AI and machine learning can provide positive benefits for teachers as well, aiding them in administrative tasks. The handwritten recognition problem mentioned in the beginning of the paper is an example of an AI tool that can help teachers with paperwork. Many teachers are buried under paperwork, which causes a decrease in their effectiveness while teaching in class. Due to this problem, about substantial number of teachers are not inspirational. Artificial intelligence can help alleviate the time spent in these time-consuming tasks, allowing them to dedicate more of their time towards the student and class. Research from McKinsey and Company gives a breakdown of the main tasks teachers perform during work. The data indicates that 51% of teacher working hours are not going towards direct student interaction but rather towards preparation, administration, and evaluation, all of which are activities that AI programs can perform. Giving teachers more time to interact with students can help with one of the primary challenges with online learning.

2.7. Student interaction

It is a common assumption that the richest learning experiences are provided by one-on-one, in-person teaching, but recent university research has offered surprising proof to the contrary. Televised course content was one of the first forms of remote learning to challenge these conceptions. Critics warned that such systems would not be able to retain students' retention, attention, focus, participation, engagement, and involvement. But the research conveyed a different message — that retention and learning through televised content was more effective than through printed material,

Ibrahim Eren Bisen
Fatih Nalcaci
Sriram Alagappan
Yetkin Yildirim

though more mental effort was required in the latter (Beentjes 1993).

Similar concerns regarding student retention have been voiced during the transition to online learning. As a result, two universities developed different AI programs to help measure a student's involvement in an online. The first method involved tracking students' mouse clicks and movements to measure their attention or distractedness. Researchers at the School of Computer Engineering and Science at Shanghai University used algorithms and programs to collect the data from an online learning system called Virtual Learning Environment (VLE) (Hussain M. et al., 2018). After collecting the data, they were able to create a machine learning algorithm that could put these data points into different patterns. The collection of the data they acquired were a combination of mouse movements, hoverings over the learning environment, and clicks on buttons in the website. After intensive sessions of training of the machine learning algorithm, the AI was able to create predictive models which they used and tested on new data to improve the quality of the predictions that the AI made (Hussain M. et al., 2018). The researchers at the university were able to correlate the predictions made by the AI to the students' overall success throughout the courses that they were taking.

The second AI-based method for measuring student engagement involved reading students' facial expressions and body language as they participated in course content in order to predict their level of participation in the classroom. Data was collected using cameras that were attached to the students' devices to analyze their engagement through AI. An academic instructor named Vladimir Soloviev from The State University of Novi Pazar created an AI that analyzes the footage from cameras around the institution to provide the university with

Ibrahim Eren Bisen
Fatih Nalcaci
Sriram Alagappan
Yetkin Yildirim

more information about the time intervals in which students are most focused in their classes. The program he developed was in a cloud feature so that it could be used with a large number of students at the same time. He conducted a multitude of tests to prove his experiments and was able to perfect his AI algorithm to have 86% accuracy with its predictions. Converting this technology for online education can help to monitor students' interaction through their camera without the need of an instructor.

These studies do not directly fix this issue of students' lack of engagement, attention, retention, focus, involvement, and engagement in a class, but they do provide a means to measure these properties in order to adjust and improve the online educational experience. More studies need to be performed to see if these methods monitor student engagement parameters, and other potential ways to measure a student's engagement. But these two approaches give an indication of AI's potential role as a supplement to instruction rather than a complete replacement of the teacher.

3. Economic effects

The rapid transition to online learning also had economic ramifications, especially for lower income families (Schellekens 2020), thus it is important to consider the economic implications of educational AI and whether it will be a detriment or a benefit. While there is not much data available regarding AI's economic impact on the education sector, research on its impact on other sectors can be used to model and infer an answer to this question. In Japan, AI has already become integral in robots and information systems, and reports show that its inclusion has brought "...increased productivity, enhanced quality, improved working environments, energy savings, and the holding down of increases in labor costs"

Ibrahim Eren Bisen
Fatih Nalcaci
Sriram Alagappan
Yetkin Yildirim

(Nagao 1986). The same report also mentions plans for computer-aided instruction in early schooling and in universities as a solution for many day-to-day tasks.

One common concern with AI is that these systems will take away jobs and lead to increased unemployment. But AI automation has caused no particular labor problems in Japan, though, it is stated that the results are mixed and that the potential for the labor-force to decline exists, but the labor problem that AI creates remedies itself because there will be a lot more jobs that are created for AI. The possible labor problem wont exist is supported by the fact that the male labor-force rate is already on a downwards trend in the United States (Furman and Seamans 2019). However, it is important to note that increased investment in AI creates more jobs and products, thus the consensus among researchers is that the impacts of AI on employment are mixed and require further study.

4. Challenges

While machine learning and AI have the potential to address some of the challenges that modern education institutions face, they do come with unique challenges of their own. Peru's Department of Education has enumerated some of these challenges in a report on the issue. The first challenge comes from the public view on AI development. People hesitate to adapt to new things they are not familiar with, and AI can be misunderstood as a force for mechanization and automation as opposed to personalization. Public policies will need to create the right ecosystem for AI that serves sustainable development. The second challenge is to ensure equity for AI in education. Developing countries still struggle to access resources and technology, making it harder for them to fund and sustain an AI education system. Before taking this approach, a basic

Ibrahim Eren Bisen
Fatih Nalcaci
Sriram Alagappan
Yetkin Yildirim

technological infrastructure must be established. The third challenge is to prepare school staff for AI and machine learning technology. Teachers must learn new digital skills if they are going to use machine learning in a meaningful way, and AI developers need to be able to communicate how school teaching systems work in order for them to be implemented effectively. The fourth challenge is to create quality data systems. AI programs require the vast collection of data in order for them to adapt and learn in real-time. This leads to the fifth challenge, which regars the ethics and transparency of data collection. AI and machine learning come with ethical concerns regarding access to personal student information, personal data, and data privacy. These five challenges will need to be addressed before any true AI revolution in education can occur.

5. Future steps

Government policies have focused on three R's when it comes to the future educational learning: relief, recovery, and rebuilding. This three R's method has been also been applicable during pandemic as well. The relief stage provides support for poor families by giving them access to necessary technologies like laptops and WiFi to ensure the student can attend online classes. This stage is where many governments are at as the technological gap between rich and poor countries remains vast (Utoikamanu). Closing this gap is the first step government and education institutions need to take in order to provide the infrastructure necessary to allow online education to succeed. The recovery stage focuses on making up for lost time. Many students learned approximately 50 percent of a usual school year curriculum during the 2020-2021 academic year, thus it is important to make up for lost time (citation here). Lastly, in the rebuilding stage, policymakers should take

Ibrahim Eren Bisen
Fatih Nalcaci
Sriram Alagappan
Yetkin Yildirim

steps to create a new system and infrastructure that can support the online education system in case another pandemic or similar situation were to occur.

6. Conclusion

The unexpected appearance of COVID-19 has caused the education sector to shift online, which has created many challenges for teachers and students alike. However, it also accelerated the development of new tools that can be utilized to make online learning more engaging and more efficient. AI-supported ELEs and ITSs make it possible to improve the education systems around the world and close the existing educational gaps between socioeconomic classes. Both artificial intelligence and machine learning technologies will drastically reduce the amount of time-consuming work that teachers must deal with and allow them to focus more of their time on student interaction. Also, with the help of ITS, students will have the opportunity to get help on topics they are having troubles with without any obstacles. It is crucial that we create the right environment for these technologies and introduce these systems to our education institutions. If we are able to allocate our resources for the improvement of artificial intelligence and machine learning in the education sector, this could result in a massive change to our struggling education systems.

References

AI Grading Tool - Online Grade Calculator for Essays, Tests |
Copyleaks. (2020). CopyLeaks.
https://copyleaks.com/education/ai-grading

Artificial Intelligence Spending Quick Look: U.S. Buying Behavior
by Industry, Company Size, and LOB Versus IT, 2020.
(2020). IDC: The Premier Global Market Intelligence
Company.
https://www.idc.com/getdoc.jsp?containerId=US47016420

AZoRobotics. (2020, November 2). Study of Students' Perception of
AI Teachers Could Help Design Better Ones.
AZoRobotics.Com.
https://www.azorobotics.com/News.aspx?newsID=11758

Beentjes, J. W., & van der Voort, T. H. (1993). Television viewing
versus reading: Mental effort, retention, and inferential
learning. *Communication Education*, *42*(3), 191-205.

Bellman, R. (1978). An introduction to artificial intelligence: can
computer think? (No. 04; Q335, B4.).

Chace, C. (2020, October 29). The Impact of Artificial Intelligence
on Education. Forbes.
https://www.forbes.com/sites/calumchace/2020/10/29/the-
impact-of-artificial-intelligence-on-education/

Chen, N., Christensen, L., Gallagher, K., Mate, R., & Rafert, G.
(2016). Global economic impacts associated with artificial
intelligence. *Analysis Group*.

Ernst, E. (2019). EconStor: Economics of artificial intelligence:
Implications for the future of work. Econstor.
https://www.econstor.eu/handle/10419/222165

Furman, J., & Seamans, R. (2019). AI and the Economy. *Innovation
policy and the economy*, *19*(1), 161-191.

George, D., Strauss, V., Meckler, L., Heim, J., & Natanson, H.
(2021, March 15). How the pandemic is reshaping
education. Washington Post.

https://www.washingtonpost.com/education/2021/03/15/pandemic-school-year-changes/

Gillham, J., Rimmington, L., Dance, H., Verweij, G., Rao, A., Roberts, K. B., & Paich, M. (2018). The macroeconomic impact of artificial intelligence. PwC Report.–PricewaterhouseCoopers.–2018.

Grother, P. J. (1995). NIST special database 19. Handprinted forms and characters database, National Institute of Standards and Technology, 10.

Guilherme, A. (2017, February 4). AI and education: the importance of teacher and student relations. AI & SOCIETY. https://link.springer.com/article/10.1007/s00146-017-0693-8?error=cookies_not_supported&code=193623eb-42fe-4e5d-a5bf-8c60742c2694

Gulzar, Z., & Leema, A. A. (2021). Machine Learning Approaches for Improvising Modern Learning Systems (Advances in Educational Technologies and Instructional Design) (1st ed.). IGI Global.

Hodges, C., Moore, S., Lockee, B., Trust, T., & Bond, A. (2020, March 27). The Difference Between Emergency Remote Teaching and Online Learning. Retrieved October 18, 2020, from https://er.educause.edu/articles/2020/3/the-difference-between-emergency-remote-teaching-and-online-learning

Holmes, W., Anastopoulou, S., Schaumburg, H., & Mavrikis, M. (2018). Technology-enhanced personalised learning: Untangling the evidence.

Holmes, W., Bialik, M., & Fadel, C. (2019). Artificial intelligence in education. Boston: Center for Curriculum Redesign.

Holstein, K. (2018, June 27). Student Learning Benefits of a Mixed-Reality Teacher Awareness Tool in. SpringerLink. https://link.springer.com/chapter/10.1007/978-3-319-93843-1_12?error=cookies_not_supported&code=34f1edc8-5245-48f7-a050-a4412dc71499

Hussain, M. (2018, October 2). Student Engagement Predictions in an e-Learning System and Their Impact on Student Course Assessment Scores. Hindawi. https://www.hindawi.com/journals/cin/2018/6347186/

Kim, J., Merrill, K., Xu, K., & Sellnow, D. D. (2020). My teacher is a machine: Understanding students' perceptions of AI teaching assistants in online education. *International Journal of Human–Computer Interaction, 36*(20), 1902-1911.

León, R. (2021, March 31). Coursera closes up 36%, topping $5.9 billion market cap in Wall Street debut. Retrieved June 17, 2021, from https://www.cnbc.com/2021/03/31/coursera-ipo-cour-begins-trading-on-the-nyse.html

Luckin, R., Holmes, W., Griffiths, M., & Forcier, L. B. (2016). Intelligence unleashed: An argument for AI in education.

Lynch, L. (2021, February 4). 4 Ways Machine Learning Can Improve Online Education. LearnDash. https://www.learndash.com/4-ways-machine-learning-can-improve-online-education/

McDermott, J. (1982). R1: A rule-based configurer of computer systems. Artificial intelligence, 19(1), 39-88.

Mayzenberg, A. (2021, June 3). Accepting and Adapting to a New Normal for School. CollegeXpress. https://www.collegexpress.com/articles-and-advice/student-life/blog/accepting-and-adapting-new-normal-school/

Murphy, R. F. (2019, January 23). Artificial Intelligence Applications to Support Teachers. Rand. https://www.rand.org/pubs/perspectives/PE315.html

Nagao, M. (1986). Social and Economic Impacts of Artificial Intelligence-A Japanese Perspective. In *Impacts of Artificial Intelligence* (pp. 99-102).

Utoikamanu, F. (n.d.). *Closing the Technology Gap in Least Developed Countries*. United Nations.

London International Conferences, 3-5 June 2021, hosted online by UKEY Consulting and Publishing, London, United Kingdom

https://www.un.org/en/chronicle/article/closing-technology-gap-least-developed-countries.

Sandoval, Z. V. (2018). Design And Implementation Of A Chatbot In Online Higher Education Settings.

Schellekens, P., & Sourrouille, D. M. (2020). COVID-19 mortality in rich and poor countries: a tale of two pandemics?. *World Bank Policy Research Working Paper*, (9260).

Soloviev, V. (2018). Machine learning approach for student engagement automatic recognition from facial expressions. SCIndeks. https://scindeks.ceon.rs/article.aspx?artid=2217-55391802079S

Soohoo, S. (2020, November). Artificial intelligence spending quick Look: U.S. buying behavior by industry, company size, and LOB Versus it, 2020. Retrieved from https://www.aws.idc.com/getdoc.jsp?containerId=US470164 20

Szczepanski, M. (2019). Economic impacts of artificial intelligence (AI). European Parliamentary Research Service (PE 637.967).

Thomas (2020, October 23). Natural Language Processing Is Changing These 5 Industries. Fast Data Science. https://fastdatascience.com/natural-language-processing-is-changing-these-5-industries/#:%7E:text=Many%20financial%20institutions%20deal%20with,document%20according%20to%20business%20requirements

UNESCO. (2019). Artificial Intelligence in Education : Challenges and opportunities for sustainable development. Working Papers on Education Policy. http://repositorio.minedu.gob.pe/handle/MINEDU/6533

Vincent-Lancrin, S., & Van der Vlies, R. (2020). Trustworthy artificial intelligence (AI) in education: Promises and challenges.

London International Conferences, 3-5 June 2021, hosted online by UKEY Consulting and Publishing, London, United Kingdom

Wladawsky-Berger, I. (2018, November 16). The Impact of
    Artificial Intelligence on the World Economy. Wall Street
    Journal.

The Agents of Socialization Keep in Touch with Socio-Virtualization

İbrahim Kurt
Stichting Cosmicus/NL

Abstract

Nowadays, while the opportunities for individuals to receive and learn what they have with their family, friends, school, and media expand, they are exposed to more human-machine interaction individually. The age of science, where we see many benefits with the advancement of technology, continues to offer many opportunities to people. Of course, what technology brings and gives must have it takes and what it carries away. It has opened new doors to the society and the individual with its contributions to socialization and individual gains. With its structure that makes the socialization tools of the society more active and affects them, it is not possible to not be affected or be under the influence of the virtual space individually and socially. Thus, the 'socialization' starts to show itself with "socio-virtualization". This situation, we encounter has begun to be studied in terms of educators, sociologists, and other fields related to this field. With the advancing technology, will a new one be added to the

London International Conferences, 3-5 June 2021, hosted online by UKEY Consulting and Publishing, London, United Kingdom

socialization tools or will it carry this function to other positions in the future? In this research, the socialization process, and the effects of technology, especially the virtual part, on society and socialization will be examined.

Keywords: Family, Friends, School, Social Media, Socialization, Socio-Virtualization

The effects of COVID 19 to private businesses in Azerbaijan

E. A. Mammadov

elman.ali.mammadov@gmail.com

I. Asadov

Abstract

It was not a surprise to hear that the COVID 19 was going to make an impact on private business all over the world. Since Azerbaijan is considered to be fairly in the "market" and its economy is slowly trying to shape up, a pandemic like this caught it off guard fractured it in certain ways. This project has been led by experienced researcher, writer, and expert in field, Ilgar Asadov. His has conducted his survey among 68 companies which are located in Absheron Peninsula (13%), Gabala (8%), Gandza (surroundings 35%), Lankaran (12%) and others (32%). Total count of employee were 4547 people. The survey respondents were 20% from manufacturing, 18.2% educational, 18.1% Food, 7.2% agricultural, 21.9% from agriculture, and 14.5% from catering industry. As per size of the businesses, 38.2% micro, 40% small, 16.3% medium and 5.5% were big enterprises.

London International Conferences, 3-5 June 2021, hosted online by UKEY Consulting and Publishing, London, United Kingdom

The survey will indicate the impacts of the pandemic from social, financial aspects. It will indicate how prepared were the enterprises and employees, how effective were the educational programs and the reaction of employees to this global crisis.

Canceled meetings, round table discussions, and plant visits have paralyzed the practical section of the education in vocational schools since the businesses were not even able to produce or the contacts in person were not allowed by governments.

The survey has also investigated changes in the dynamics of the businesses, shifts and agility of the culture in the companies as well direction they are heading in the future. It will also suggest certain solutions and possible recovery plan for those are deeply impacted.

At the end, we will see the expert's approach, analysis and expectations about the subject.

Keywords: Private economy, small businesses, micro business, medium enterprise, big enterprises, home office, impacts of COVID

Economic Impact of Diaspora Remittance on Nigerian Economy

Benedict Ebenezer Alechenu
Technical University Kosice
benedict.ebenezer.alechenu@tuke.sk

Abstract

The purpose of this paper is to assess the huge impact of Diaspora remittance on the Nigerian economy. In 2018, migrant remittances to Nigeria were $24.3 billion, representing 6.1% of gross domestic product. This figure represents 83% of the Federal Government budget in 2018 and 11 times the Foreign Direct Investment (FDI) flows in same period. Remittances are the fastest growing source of foreign exchange earnings in Nigeria. Hence in March 2021, as part of its reforms to boost the inflow of foreign currency in the country, the Central Bank of Nigeria (CBN) introduced an incentive of N5 for every $1 of fund remitted to Nigeria through International Money Transfer Organisations in its forex policy. Remittances, or money transfers, make up the

London International Conferences, 3-5 June 2021, hosted online by UKEY Consulting and Publishing, London, United Kingdom

second-largest source of foreign exchange receipts after oil revenue in Nigeria, Africa's biggest economy. $24.8billion was sent to Nigeria in 2019, according to the World Bank data.

Keyword: Diaspora, Economic development, Remittance

London International Conferences, 3-5 June 2021, hosted online by UKEY Consulting and Publishing, London, United Kingdom

1.Introduction

A Remittance is generally meant to be money sent to another party/person usually one in another country. The sender is typically a foreign worker and the recipient a relative back home. A remittance is a payment of money that is transferred to another party. Broadly speaking, any payment of an invoice or a bill can be called a remittance. However, the term is mostly used nowadays to describe a sum of money sent by someone working abroad to his or her family back home.

Remittance can be viewed as funds transferred from migrants to their home country, such funds played vital roles in the economy, helping to meet the basic needs of recipients. Most remittances are made by foreign workers to family members in their home countries. The most common way of making a remittance is by using an electronic payment system through a bank or a money transfer service such as Western Union, Ria money transfer, money gram etc. People who use these options are generally charged a fee. Transfers can take as little as ten minutes to reach the recipient. remittances represent household income from foreign economies arising mainly from the temporary or permanent movement of people to those economies.

Remittances are transfers of money, goods and diverse traits by migrants or migrant groups back to their countries of origin. Although nowadays, the notion of remittances conjures only monetary aspect, remittances includes both monetary and non-monetary flows, including social remittances.

Diaspora remittances have played, and it is still playing a major role on Nigerian economy at large, hence in March 2021, the Central Bank of Nigeria made it crystal clear that it

London International Conferences, 3-5 June 2021, hosted online by UKEY Consulting and Publishing, London, United Kingdom

is of a national interest to make policy that will encourage those in diaspora to send money back home to their relatives without many hurdles. In fact, the Central Bank of Nigeria has put in place a well functional mechanism and incentives that will augment free flow of remittances to the country.

In March 2021, as part of its reforms to boost the inflow of foreign currency in the country, the CBN introduced an incentive of N5 for every $1 of fund remitted to Nigeria through International Money Transfer Organisations in its forex policy. And according to the Punch of 6th May 2021, the Central Bank of Nigeria (CBN) extends naira-4-dollar scheme deadline indefinitely. The Central bank of Nigeria has declared unequivocally that it is hell bent to ease the barriers faced by those in diaspora in sending money back home to their friends and family.

According to the Central Bank Governor Mr Godwin Emefiele, "the reforms were introduced because increased diaspora remittances into the country would support the economy and help reduce the impact of the COVID-19 pandemic on the Nigerian economy".

Rising dollar demand has been putting pressure on the naira. Nigeria is hoping it can attract remittances from its Diaspora as providers of foreign exchange, many offshore investors, have exited after COVID-19 triggered a fall in oil prices.

Remittances, or money transfers, make up the second-largest source of foreign exchange receipts after oil revenues in Nigeria, Africa's biggest economy. More than $24 billion was sent to Nigeria in 2019, according to the World Bank.

London International Conferences, 3-5 June 2021, hosted online by UKEY Consulting and Publishing, London, United Kingdom

Among the Nigerian commercial banks that have keyed into the central bank's vision of increasing diaspora remittances via the formal channel are: United Bank for Africa (UBA). ECO bank Plc, First bank Nigeria Plc, Keystone bank Nigeria Plc, Zenith bank Nigeria Plc etc. UBA has introduced a bouquet of products that would accelerate remittances, transfers, trade, and commerce into and from Nigeria in particular, and Africa in general. Several other banks have keyed into the CBN's vision.

2. Background of Study

Diaspora or Migrant remittance has been in existence in the World for decades; it is as old as globalisation, and it has been modernised since the 21st century.

A **remittance** is a non-commercial transfer of money by a foreign worker, a member of a diaspora community, or a citizen with family ties abroad, for household income in their home country or homeland. Money sent home by migrants competes with international aid as one of the largest financial inflows to developing countries. Workers' remittances are a significant part of international capital flows, especially regarding labour-exporting countries.

2.1 World remittances

According to the World Bank, in 2018 overall global remittance grew by 10% to US$689 billion in 2017, with developing countries receiving 77% or US$528 billion. India, China, Mexico, the Philippines, and Egypt are among the largest remittance recipients globally, collectively accounting for approximately 36% of total inflows.

According to World Bank, global remittances declined sharply by about 20 percent in 2020 due to the economic crisis induced by the COVID-19 pandemic and shutdown. The fall was the sharpest decline in recent history, largely due to a fall in the wages and employment of migrant workers, who tend to be more vulnerable to loss of employment and wages during an economic crisis in a host country. Remittances to low and middle-income countries (LMICs) fell by 19.7 percent to $445 billion, representing a loss of a crucial financing lifeline for many vulnerable households.

The Global Director of the Social Protection and Jobs Global Practice at the World Bank, Mr. Michal Rutkowski, recently highlighted the importance of remittance flows to the financial survival of families that were stricken by the impact of COVID-19 pandemic disease that plagued the world economy in 2020.

Rutkowski, said in the World Bank's report titled: "Defying Predictions, Remittance Flows Remain Strong During COVID-19 Crisis,'" he said that "as COVID-19 still devastates families around the world, remittances continue to provide a critical lifeline for the poor and vulnerable. Supportive policy responses, together with national social protection systems, should continue to be inclusive of all communities, including migrants." In view of this kind of unforeseeable challenges, the G7 has put in place a working strategy to reduce the cost of remittances to avoid the aim been defeated.

The World Bank's release also stated that Nigeria accounted for 40 per cent of remittance flows into Sub-Saharan Africa in 2020 by receiving over $17 billion out of inflow of $44 billion to Africa. This is pretty much understandable because of the high number of Nigerians in diaspora, partly because of its population when compared to countries in the Sub-Saharan Africa.

3: Methodology Applied

Secondary data were used to analyse the economic impact of Diaspora remittance on Nigerian economy. In addition, a comparative analysis of some various countries' remittances was used to give a more precise view on the impact of diaspora remittances around the globe. The data used for the analyses were obtained from Worldbank.org/indicator for selected countries that have the highest remittances in the World.

Table:1 Personal remittances, received current USD in billions between 2014-2020

country/region	2014	2015	2016	2017	2018	2019	2020
Nigeria	20.99	20.62	19.69	22.03	24.31	23.8	17.2
Sub-Saharan Africa	39.68	42.19	38.61	42.33	48.16	48	44
World	470	596	589	633	689	714	702
China	29.91	44.44	35.22	28.67	24.30	18.29	60
Egypt	19.57	18.32	18.59	24.73	25.51	26.78	24
India	70.39	68.91	62.74	68.96	78.79	83.33	76
Mexico	24.80	26.23	28.69	32.27	35.76	39.02	41
Philippines	28.69	29.79	31.14	32.81	33.80	35.16	33.2

Source: https://data.worldbank.org/indicator/BX.TRF.PWKR.DT.GD.ZS

The above table on personal remittances, received current USD in billions showed the top five countries with the highest remittances in the World during the year under review.

Table:2 personal remittances, received as a percentage of GDP in billions between 2014-20120

Country/region	Indicator % of GDP	2014	2015	2016	2017	2018	2019
Nigeria	remittances	3.84	4.23	4.86	5.86	6.12	5.31
Sub-Saharan Africa	remittances	2.24	2.57	2.49	2.59	2.78	2.76
World	remittances	0.72	0.77	0.74	0.74	0.75	0.76
China	remittances	0.29	0.40	0.31	0.23	0.17	0.13
Egypt	remittances	6.40	5.56	5.59	10.49	10.22	8.84
India	remittances	3.45	3.28	2.73	2.6	2.90	2.91
Mexico	remittances	1.89	2.24	2.66	2.79	2.93	3.08
Philippines	remittances	9.64	9.72	9.77	9.99	9.75	9.33

Source: https://data.worldbank.org/indicator/BX.TRF.PWKR.DT.GD.ZS

Table:3 Personal remittances, received current USD in billions by selected countries in the Sub-Saharan countries in 2020

Country name	Indicator	Year
Nigeria	remittances	17.2
Ethiopia	remittances	3.7
Ghana	remittances	3.6
Kenya	remittances	3.1
Senegal	remittances	2.6
Zimbabwe	remittances	1.2
Uganda	remittances	1.1
Mali	remittances	1

Source: https://data.worldbank.org/indicator/BX.TRF.PWKR.DT.GD.ZS

4. Data analysis and Results

Data were carefully analysed and interpreted using graphs for more comprehensiveness and clarities. The use of graphs added more in-depth analysis and interpretations. The translation of data into graphs give us a clearer understanding of the results obtained, because data analysis is the backbone of most academic research.

Fig:1 A 2-D Line chart showing personal remittances, received current USD 2014-2020

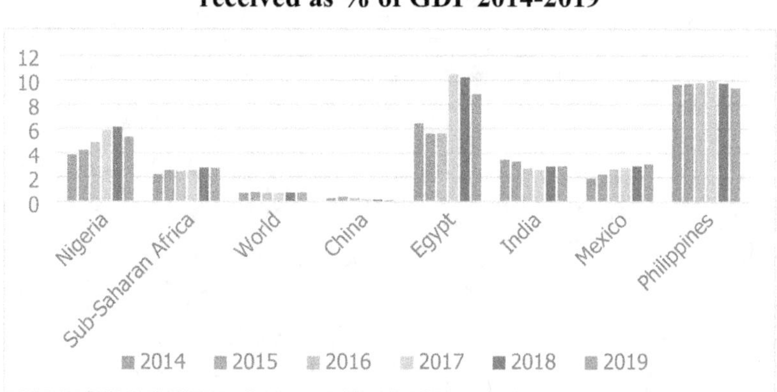

Source: Own source

During the period under review, remittances to Nigeria were relatively stable when compared to the number of Diasporas from India and China. It is due in part because of the monetary policy put in place by Central Bank of Nigeria.

Fig.2 A clustered Column Chart showing personal remittances, received as % of GDP 2014-2019

Source: Own source

During the period under review, Egypt has the highest remittances as the percentage of its GDP in 20217 and 2018 respectively; followed by Philippines. Nigeria has its highest remittances as a percentage of its GDP in 2018. Nigeria remittances as a percentage of its GDP grew continuously from 2014-2018 and declined in 2019. China has the least remittances as the percentage of its GDP throughout the period under investigation.

Fig.3 Personal remittances, received current USD in billions by selected countries in Sub-Saharan Africa in 2020

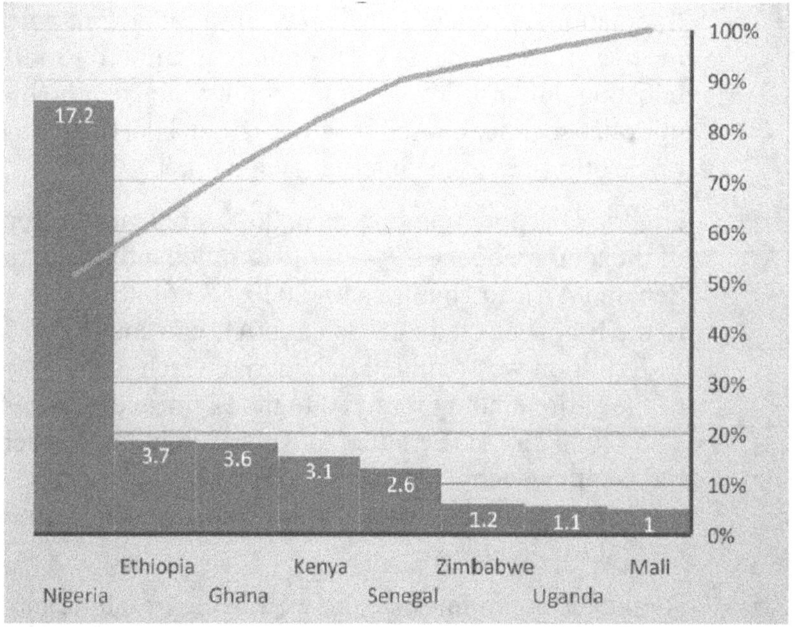

Source: Own source

Among the selected Sub-Saharan African countries, remittance to Nigeria in 2020 was more than half of the remittances to the rest of the five countries. Remittances to Nigeria in 2020 was

$17.2 billion, which is a significant amount that added enormous value to the economy.

5. Conclusion and Recommendations

Diaspora remittance is very paramount to Nigeria economic development, it is the second largest foreign exchange inflows into the country. Based on this fact, in March 2021, the Central Bank of Nigeria has put in place an unhindered policy measure that warrant an easy smooth Diaspora remittance into the country. It has introduced a generous rebate titled "N5 for $1" meaning that for every $1 remitted to Nigeria through International Money Transfer organisation, the recipient will receive an additional N5. This policy is tailored toward boosting dollar inflows into the country, to cushion the effect of dollar scarcity caused by covid-19 lockdown and the fall of crude oil prices at the international market.

Nigeria Diaspora remittances in 2020 stood at $17.2billion out of the total amount of $44billion remitted into the entire Sub-Saharan African countries. In 2020, $33.5billion was remitted to the Eight selected Sub-Saharan African countries, $17.2billion was remitted to Nigeria, which is more than half of the entire amount remitted to the Eight selected countries. The actual amount remitted to Nigeria might be higher, due to the fact the Central Bank of Nigeria's lack of methods to measure informal/unofficial ways through which remittances enter the country.

Remittances can improve the well-being of family members left behind and boost the economies of receiving countries.

Remittances can also create a culture of dependency in the receiving country, lowering labour force participation, promoting conspicuous consumption, and slowing economic growth.

London International Conferences, 3-5 June 2021, hosted online by UKEY Consulting and Publishing, London, United Kingdom

6. Recommendations

Central Bank of Nigeria (CBN) should encourage those in diaspora to open online naira account without much hazzles. The CBN should provide incentives to commercials banks that would encourage them to send their staff abroad to provide Bank Verification Number (BVN) services/registration to those in Diaspora.

London International Conferences, 3-5 June 2021, hosted online by UKEY Consulting and Publishing, London, United Kingdom

Bibliography

Aelex, I, E. (2020). Diaspora remittances in Nigeria: Examining the new CBN policy. https://www.mondaq.com/nigeria/financial-services/diaspora-remittances

Africa Check. (2021). How many Nigerians Abroad? How much cash do they send home? https://africacheck.org/fact-checks/reports/how-many-nigerians-abroad-and-how-much-cash-do-they-send-home.

DAILY NEWS. (2021). Official Remittances to Nigeria Plummet by Almost 40% in a year When Crypto Used Surged

Ethiopian Diaspora Agency (2021). Ethiopian Diaspora Remits $1.4 in Five Months. https://www.amchamethiopia.org/post/ethiopian-diaspora-remits-1-4-billion-in-five- months

Johnbrowne, A, O. (2020). Diaspora remittances and Nigeria's economic growth. BusinessDay Newspaper. https://businessday.ng/opinion/article/diaspora-remittances-and-nigerias-economic-growth

Kalantaryan, S; Mcmahon, S. (2020). Covid-19 and remittances in Africa. European Commission. JRC Technical Report

Komolafe, B. (2021). Diaspora Cash Remittance s Drop by 27% to $17.2 billion. Vanguard. https://www.vanguardngr.com/diaspora-cash-remittances-drop-by-27-to-17-2bn

McCarthy, N. (2021). The World's Top Remittance Recipients. Https://www.statista.com/ chart/20166/top-10-remittance-receiving-countries

Norrestad, F. (2021). Values of remittances sent to Sub-Saharan Africa in 2020, by countryin billions of U.S. dollars. https://www.statista.com/statistics/962857/remittances-to-sub-saharan-african-countries

Nweze, C. (2021). Diaspora remittances drop by $4.65billion. The Nation Newspaper.

Oluwafemi, A; Ayandibu, A, O. (2017). Impact of remittances on development in Nigeria: Challenges and prospects. Journal of Sociology and Social Anthropology, 5:3,311,318

Onwuamaeze, D. (2021). Driving Remittance Flows in Africa. THISDAY Newspaper

Osemenshan, A, F. (2019). Remittances and Economic growth nexus in Nigeria: Does financial sector development play a critical role? International Journal of Management, Economics, and social sciences (IJMESS). https://www.econstor.eu/bitstream

Pew Research Centre. (2017). Strength from Abroad: the economic power of Nigeria's Diaspora. https://www.pwc.com/ng/en/pdf/the-economic-power-of-nigerias-diaspora

Reuters. (2021). Nigeria extends naira incentive offer to boost Diaspora inflow.

Thorne, T. (2021). Historic Amount of money sent to Mexico in 2020. https://www.kpbs.org/news/2021/mar/23/historic-amount-remittances-sent-mexico-2020

Trading Economics. (2008-2020 data). Nigeria remittances. https://tradingeconomics.com/nigeria/remittances

Usim, U. (2021). Nigeria, others recorded $540 billion remittances flows in 2020-World Bank. THE SUN

World Bank. (2019). Personal remittances, received as a % of GDP. https://data.worldbank.org/indicator/BX.TRF.PWKR.DT.GD.ZS=2019chart

World Bank Group; Knomad (2019). Migration and Remittances: Recent Development and Outlook

Global Migration Data. (2021). Remittances Data. https://migrationdataportal.org/themes/remittances

London International Conferences

londonic.uk

UKEY
CONSULTING & PUBLISHING

ukeyconsultingpublishing.co.uk

Employment Reduction as A Factor of Consumer Debt Growth in the Covid-19 Pandemic

Nosova Olga

Doctor of Economic Sciences, V.N. Karazin Kharkiv National University

https://orcid.org/0000-0002-5638-6294

olgano59@gmail.com

Abstract

The article's main goal is to analyse the decline in employment effects on the growth of consumer debt in the COVID-19 pandemic. Evaluating various approaches for employment decrease effect on the consumer debt rise proved the necessity of assessing the impact of economic performance and country-specific factors. The study by Dingel & Neiman (2020) shows that 38 % for high-income economies and only 13 % for low-income countries can work from home. Assuming there is a linear relationship between the share of people who can work from home and the country's GDP, this share for Ukraine stands at about 20 %. Stay-at–home orders caused business closures and were accompanied by the decline in demand for travel, accommodations, restaurants, entertainment, and in other industries. The restrictive measures led to a significant reduction in employment and a loss of income in many countries' households in the world. The dramatic decline of economic activity, contraction of production, unemployment rise, and a drop of labour productivity produce employment income losses due to the spread of COVID 19. UN OCHA in Ukraine (2021) reports that since the beginning of the pandemic, more than 80% of households have lost income and in more than 40% of families, at least one family member has lost her/his job. Ukraine has introduced partial moratorium-releasing debtors from liability for the delayed performance of obligations under consumer loans.

In the context of presenting approaches, a number of significant conclusions were drawn, proving full shut up measures for localization disease dissemination. The imposition of restrictions on the working life, the introduction of new remote forms of work and education proposes a special policy, which depends on the national economic and financial potential. The health system development and adoption stabilization measures of the epidemic situation in the country are the basis to restore confidence and trust in the society.

Empirical analyses conducted on the results of a survey carried out among employees in Ukraine. The assessment survey results based on the questionnaires of the quality of debt advice services for European households. The study sampled 100 respondents in various spheres of activity in June 2020. The results of respondent analysis have found that the consumer debt increased in the lockdown period from March to June 2020, and a significant number of SMEs shut up. Different types of consumer debt – consisting of mortgages, credit cards, auto loans have risen. Many Ukrainians have lost income and faced financial hardships. The observations illustrate that significant changes are reflecting the uncertainty upsurge in society, over-indebtedness increases in a hotel, restaurant, tourist industries, retail and wholesale trade. The number of households' over-indebted rises over the past 10 years has increased in Ukraine. Survey result suggest that since March 2020 to June 2020 poverty rate will increase.

The article pays attention to the possible threats to the Ukrainian economy through protracted extension and strengthening of domestic quarantine measures, lack of a clear action plan to support low-income citizens, and economic downfall of economic activity due to the COVID-19 pandemic. The article suggests the government support the population, provide financial aid to the most vulnerable populations, and exempt the persons having lost their jobs from repayment of mortgage loans on a temporary basis, until the end of the year, without imposing a fine or accruing interest. Adoption of the program for SMEs and to the most damaged industries development will restore the confidence and trust of entrepreneurs in future business activities. The research proves a need to increase the relevant share of debt advice services and quality.

Keywords: employment, consumer debt, households, over-indebtedness, debt advice services.

London International Conferences

londonic.uk   ukeyconsultingpublishing.co.uk

The Impact of African Continental Free Trade Agreement

Benedict Ebenezer Alechenu
Technical University Kosice
benedict.ebenezer.alechenu@tuke.sk

Abstract

The birth of African Continental Free Trade agreement which came into effect on the 1st of January 2021, has a huge positive impact on the continent. The implementation has brought about enormous economic growth in African countries. African Continental Free Trade agreement is the World largest trade bloc since the creation of World Trade Organisation in 1994. It has united 1.3billion people and with annual trade potential of over \$4trillion. The implementation of AfCFTA has increased the movement of people across the subregion ahead of the planned/envisaged introduction of continental passport. In all paradigms, AfCFTA has unlocked the growth and development potentials tied down for decades. This is a gigantic step toward the actualisation of the four-cardinal principle/pillar laid down by the founding fathers of the African Union, which are: Economic, political, social, and technological integration. The unity of African countries depends solely on their economic integration brought about by the implement of AfCFTA. This is the vehicle that will take

African continent out of the abject poverty, under-development, and low standard of living. The free trade agreement is a win-win for all the African countries. It has boosted, trading activities, production capacity, employment aggregate and income gains on the continent.

Keywords: Economic development, free-trade agreement, Economic integration

1. Introduction

A landmark free-trade agreement removing most tariffs and other commercial barriers in the African continent came into effect on the 1st of January 2021, as 54 sovereign member states agreed to implement the accord. The African Free Trade Agreement commits the governments to greater economic integration, as the signatory states begin a multiyear process to remove trade barriers including tariffs on 90% of commodities and reduce non-tariff barriers. The duty-free movement of goods is expected to boost regional trade, while also helping countries move away from mainly exporting raw materials and build manufacturing capacity to attract foreign investment. African countries are the major exporters of raw materials and the least exporters of finished products. The launching and implementation of the Continental Free Trade Agreement is one of the major processes toward actualisation of the pan-Africanism integration imbedded on the core value of the African Unity.

It is worthy to note that the implementation of the African Continental Free Trade Agreement is the spring bud to African economic transformation to the World next economic miracle. African leaders should make it a topmost priority by implementing the agreement in full to break colonial trade barriers and promote intra-regional trade, which is the only way African continent can develop and speak in one voice at the World stage and during multi-lateral agreement. African leaders must grab without delay the golden opportunities offered by AfCFTA that is geared towards encouraging African countries to trade more among themselves instead of other parts of the World. AfCFTA would enable African countries to industrialize and focus on manufacturing instead of exporting raw materials which attract meagre profits.

Africa needs not only a trade policy, but also a continental manufacturing agenda, the vision for intra-African trade is for the free movement of made-in-Africa goods. That is, goods and services

London International Conferences, 3-5 June 2021, hosted online by UKEY Consulting and Publishing, London, United Kingdom

made locally with dominant African content in terms of raw materials and value addition.

African Continental Free Trade Agreement should not only create wealth for investors, but also prosperity for Africans. The benefits of economic growth must be prosperity for the masses, that would transform the continent into the World economic hub, considering the fact, that the continent is enormously endowed with both human and material resources.

2. Background of Study

The roots of the AfCFTA can be traced back to the 1980 Lagos Plan of Action and a plan in 1991 to launch the African Economic Community (AEC). Neither of these were implemented but the goal remained much alive. The launching of the AfCFTA is considered as the most crucial step towards the economic integration among the African countries. African leaders have demonstrated that the continent can only achieve its developmental goals through massive intra-regional trade among the 54 African countries without barrier (barrier free)

The first phase of the agreement was adopted and signed by the African Union Heads of State and governments at its 10th Extraordinary Summit in Kigali, Rwanda, on March 21, 2018. The AfCFTA treaty is one of the flagship initiatives of the African Union Agenda 2063, aimed at creating a single continental market for goods and services, with free movement of businesspersons, investments, and the hope of creating a single currency across the continent.

There are five major sub-regional economic integration arrangements that encompasses all the countries in Africa. These are: *the Arab Maghreb Union* (AMU); *The Common Market of Eastern and Southern Africa* (COMESA); *The Economic Community of Central African States* (ECCAS); *The Economic Community of West African States* (ECOWAS); and the *Southern African Development Community* (SADC).

London International Conferences, 3-5 June 2021, hosted online by UKEY Consulting and Publishing, London, United Kingdom

The various regional community blocs have common objectives. In West Africa, ECOWAS since its formation on May 28th, 1975, it has had the objective of constructing a free trade area among member states. ECOWAS is a regional political and economic union of fifteen countries located in West Africa. Collectively, these countries comprise an area of 5,114,162 km^2, population of over 381,91million.

The Southern African Development Community (SADC) was established in 1992 and the **SADC Free Trade Area** (FTA) came into being in 2008. The FTA were made up of 13 member countries out of the region's 15 countries (Angola and the DRC have not signed up) but only five countries are members of the **Southern African Customs Union** (SACU), Botswana, Eswatini, Lesotho, Namibia, and South Africa. The SACU was formed in 1910.

The Arab Maghreb Union (AMU) was formed in 1989 by Algeria, Libya, Mauritania, Morocco, and Tunisia as a vehicle to promote economic and political integration among member states.

The Common Market for Eastern and Southern Africa (COMESA) was formed in December 1994 to replace the former Preferential Trade Area (PTA) from the early 1980s in Eastern and Southern Africa. COMESA was created to serve as an organization of free independent sovereign States that have agreed to cooperate in developing their natural and human resources for the good of all their people. In this context, the focus of COMESA has been on the formation of a large economic and trading unit to overcome trade barriers faced by individual States. The objectives of COMESA reflect its priorities to promote sustainable economic development.

The Economic Community of Central African states (ECCAS) was established on October 1983, with the aims of promoting and strengthening a harmonious cooperation in order to realize a balanced and self-sustained economic development,

London International Conferences, 3-5 June 2021, hosted online by UKEY Consulting and Publishing, London, United Kingdom

particularly in the fields of industry, transport and communications, energy, agriculture, natural resources, trade, customs, monetary and financial matters, human resources, tourism, education, culture, science and technology and the movement of persons with a view to achieving collective self-reliance, raising the standards of living, maintaining economic stability and fostering peaceful relations between the member States and contributing to the development of the African continent.

Some of the Africa's Regional Economic Communities (RECs) have gone some way to achieving integration. Larger countries within an individual REC have tended to become a centre for trading, using the relationships they have with fellow members. Kamal Nasrollah, Partner and Head of the law firm Baker McKenzie in Casablanca has studied this phenomenon and believes that the AfCFTA could use the example of these Regional Economic Communities (RECs). He cites Ivory Coast, Kenya, Senegal, and South Africa and gives some detail on the Moroccan experience.

3. Methodology Applied

In this article, Secondary dada were used to get an overview of the volume of intra-regional trade among regions in the World, we collected data from World Integrated Trade Solution (WITS) for a comprehensive analysis. This is quite imperative for us to know how regions in the World conduct trading activities within their subregion. African intra-regional trade is the key success factor to the African continental free trade agreement which came into effect on the 1st of January 2021. We used data from 2014 -2018 and compared it with the volume of trade among the regions.

Table: 1 Regional trade in percentage of their GDP 2014-2018

Country/Region	Indicator Name	2014	2015	2016	2017	2018
Sub-Saharan Africa	Trade in % of GDP	57.95	53.17	50.63	50.87	53.63
East Asia & Pacific	Trade in % of GDP	63.40	58.16	54.30	56.63	58.03
Europe & Central Asia	Trade in % of GDP	79.60	80.21	79.59	82.59	84.09
Latin America & Caribbean	Trade in % of GDP	43.30	47.67	44.67	45.29	46.84
Middle East & North Africa	Trade in % of GDP	84.45	79.92	75.70	79.50	86.24
North America	Trade in % of GDP	33.11	31.24	30.04	30.59	31.05
South Asia	Trade in % of GDP	47.29	41.10	39.11	39.55	42.08

Source: World Integrated Trade Solution (WITS)

4. Results and Analysis

In this section, results of the findings are thoroughly analysed
with the use of graphs. The graphs enable us to have a precise
and concise interpretation of the volume of intra-regional trade
in the various sub-regions. Results collected were used to
compare and contrast the level of intra-regional trade among
the sub-regional groups. Data were tabulated to give us a
clearer picture of how sub-regions integrate economically
through trade and investments.

**Fig.1 A Clustered Column Chart Showing the volume of
trade among African countries between 2014-2018**

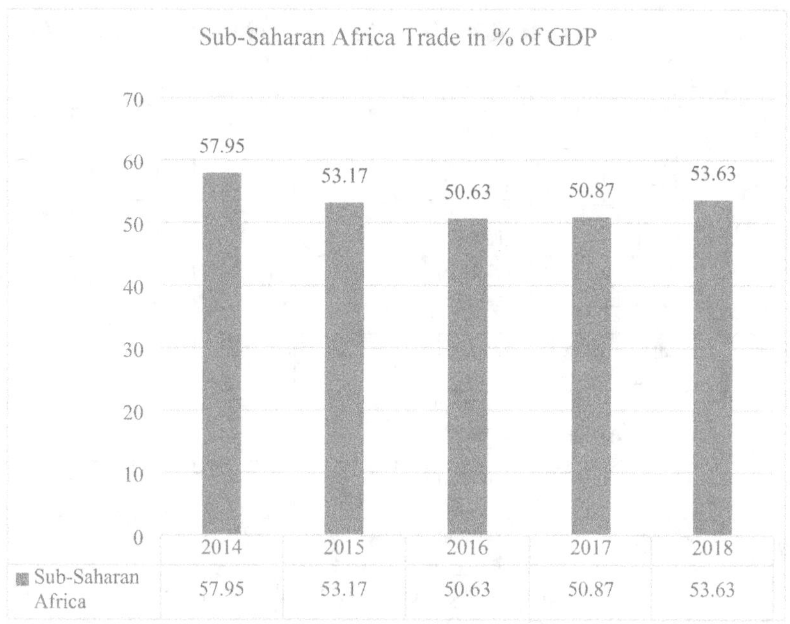

Source: Own source

During the period under investigation, the sub-Saharan Africa countries witnessed the highest trade in percentage of GDP in 2014, which is a clear evidence that the volume of intra-regional trade was at its best. There was a sharp decrease in the volume of trade in 2015 and 2016, respectively. While in 2017, the percentage of trade to GDP increased gradually to the tone of 0.24%. The Sub-Saharan Africa trade in percentage of GDP increased rapidly from 50.87 to 53.63, which is a sign of high volume of trading activities among the countries in the sub-region.

Fig.2: Clustered Bar Chart showing the seven intra-regional trade as a % of GDP between 2014-2018

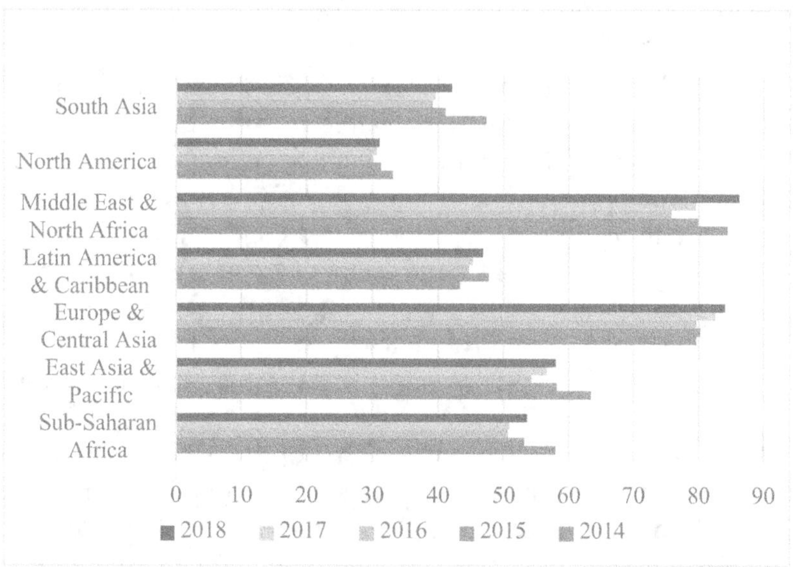

During the period under review, Middle East and North Africa Sub-region have the highest intra-regional trade as a percentage of GDP in 2018, followed by Europe and Central Asia with the trade volume of 86.24 and 84.09, respectively. As shown on the above Clustered Bar chart, the two most integrated regions in terms of intra-regional trade were Middle East & North Africa and Europe and Central Asia.

During the period under study, Sub-Saharan Africa witnessed its highest volume of trade in 2014 to the tone of 57.95 as the percentage of its GDP.

Among the regions under investigation between 2014 to 2018, North America witnessed the lowest volume of intra-regional trade as the percentage of its GDP. This is partly because United States of America and Canada which are the two biggest economies in the sub-region conduct most of their trading activities outside the subregion. Another factor is the huge size of USA GDP.

London International Conferences, 3-5 June 2021, hosted online by UKEY Consulting and Publishing, London, United Kingdom

5. Conclusion

The recently launched African Continental Free Trade
Agreement is the most viable way the dreams of the founding
Fathers of African Union can be actualised in no distant time.
The prime or overarching objective behind the AfCFTA is the
elimination or reduction of tariff and non-tariff barriers
amongst the 54 Countries that agreed to be members of the
bloc by providing a single market for goods and services,
facilitated by movement of persons to deepen the economic
integration and prosperity. The formation of AfCFTA is the
African continent's most ambitious integration initiative,
embedded in the agenda 2063 of the African Union, whose
main objective is to create a single continental market for
goods and services with free movement of people and
investments, thus expanding intra-African trade across the
continent. With the birth of AfCFTA, investors can now enjoy
both freedom of establishment and freedom of services within
the continent. Currently, the volume of intra-regional trade in
Africa is low compared to the European continent; but with the
launch of AfCFTA, and its full implementations, the volume of
intra-regional trade in Africa will increase to propel
development and eradicate poverty on the continent.

AfCFTA is expected to increase intra-Africa trade from an
existing level of about 13% to 25% or more through better
harmonisation and coordination of trade liberalisation. This
will be driven forward by the complementary Single African
Air Transport Market and the Protocol on Free Movement of
Persons. AfCFTA is expected to unlock the locked, to tap the
untapped human and material resources through trade
liberalisation and abolition of barriers to trade.

The share of intra-African trade remained low, unlocking
Africa's full economic potential would require economic
integration from all sides; globally, regionally, as well as the
rural and urban areas.

London International Conferences, 3-5 June 2021, hosted online by UKEY
Consulting and Publishing, London, United Kingdom

The Impact of African Continental Free Trade agreement

B. E. Alechenu

London International Conferences, 3-5 June 2021, hosted online by UKEY Consulting and Publishing, London, United Kingdom

References

African Development Bank Group. (2020). Regional integration, Trade, and Investment

Africa Regional Integration Index. (2019). Report. https://www.integrate-africa.org/fileadmin/

Adekoya, F. (2019). Activate safeguards after AfCFTA ratification, operators tell FG. The Guardian

Akamanzi, C. (2006). "Land locked to land linked' 2005". ILEAP Trade facilitation Program.

Balima, B. (2019). UPDATE 1-Economic "game changer"? African leaders launch free trade zone. Reuters

Brown, A, O. 2019. Nigeria's Buhari Says Made-in-Africa Key to Success of Free-Trade Deal. Bloomberg

Cariière, C. (2004). "African Regional Agreements: Impact on Trade with or without Currency Union." Journal of African Economies, 13(2): 199-239

Daka, T; Adekoya, F; Ibirogba, F; Agboluaje, R. (2019). How to make Africa's free trade deal work for Nigeria. The Guardian

De Melo, J; Wagner; L. (2016). "Aid for Trade and the Trade Facilitation Agreement: What They Can Do for LDCs." Journal of World Trade 50(6): 935–69

GCA (2006) "Report of the Mission of GCA Eminent Persons on Regional Integration in West Africa: Towards Rationalization and Increased Efficiency" GLOBAL COALITION FOR AFRICA, Washington DC

Hoije, K. (2019). African Trade Pact Starts Operations With 54 Signatories. Bloomberg

Hoije, K. (2019). African Union Landmark Trade Pact Grows, as Benin, Nigeria Join. Bloomberg

International Monetary Fund. (2005). Regional Economic Outlook Sub-Saharan Africa"

Lewis, J.D; Robinson; S; Thierfelder; K. (2003). "Free Trade
       Agreements and the SADC Economies." Journal of African
       Economies 2: 156-2006

Lungo, L. (2019). The African Continental Free Trade Area: The
       Role of EU Support for Africa's Historic Trade Agreement.
       /www.oegfe.at/policy-briefs/the-african-continental-free-
       trade-area

Miriri, D. (2019). EXPLAINER-Africa to decide on free-trade zone:
       what is at stake? Reuters

Njinkeu,D; Powo,F, B. (2006). Intra-African Trade and Regional
       Integration.
       https://www.researchgate.net/publication/228615205

Ogalue, L. (2019). Africa's total merchandise trade stands at
       $997.9bn. Nigeria News Headlines Today

Onuah, F. (2019). West African states adopt flexible FX regime for
       regional trade. Reuters

Otaru, A. (2019). Group targets $1 trillion to eliminate Leadership
       unemployment in Nigeria. The Guardian

Oyebade,W. (2019). West Africa targets $57b investment, integrated
       ports, rail sector. Guardian Newspaper

Oyejide, A., Elbadawi, I; Yeo, S. (1999) Regional Integration and
       Trade Liberalization in SubSaharan Africa, Volume 3,
       Regional Case Studies. Macmillan Press Ltd

Sahara Reporters. (2019). Nigerian Government Doesn't Understand
       Continental Free Trade Area "CFTA" Agreement -AfDB

Salau, S. (2019). Nigeria, Benin Customs adopt single goods
       declaration procedure. The Guardian

Summary of intra-Africa trade. 2019.
       https://www.tralac.org/documents/publications/trade-data-
       analysis/3982-summary-intra-africa-trade-2019

The Guardian Newspaper. (2019). ECOWAS restates commitment
       to free trade, new opportunities.

London International Conferences, 3-5 June 2021, hosted online by UKEY
Consulting and Publishing, London, United Kingdom

The Nation Newspaper. (2019). AfCFTA will be world's largest free trade area, says AfDB.

Udo, B. (2019). Why Nigeria will not rush into African free trade agreement – Buhari. Premium Times

United Nations Conference on Trade and Development (2019). Economic Development in Africa Report 2019. Made in Africa – Rules of Origin for Enhanced Intra-African

Vollgraaf, R. (2019). Nigeria Will Sign African Free-Trade Pact at AU Meeting in Niger. Bloomberg

WITS Data worldbank.org (2014-2018). Sub-Saharan Africa Trade in % of GDP.

https://dataportal.opendataforafrica.org/

https://wits.worldbank.org/CountryProfile/en/Country/SSF/StartYear/2014/EndYear/2018/Indicator/NE-TRD-GNFS-ZS

https://tradingeconomics.com/country-list/exports?continent=africa

London International Conferences

londonic.uk

ukeyconsultingpublishing.co.uk

Organization Structure and Management Practice Related Factors Causing Heavy Workload: An Empirical Study Among Sanitary Workers

Durairaj Rajan

Department of Business Administration, Faculty of Social and Management Sciences, University of Africa, Toru-Orua, Bayelsa State, Nigeria

drdirajan@gmail.com

Abstract

This survey, quantitative and empirical based descriptive research has the objective of analysing perception of sanitary workers working in private multi-speciality hospitals in Tirunelveli city of Tamil Nadu, India towards various organization structure and management practice related factors causing heavy workload. In order to achieve the objective, the study sampled 80 respondents using both convenience and judgement sampling techniques; and from the chosen respondents the primary data were collected using schedule method with the help of questionnaire (translating the questions in respondents' mother language, 'Tamil') along with interview. The secondary data were collected from

London International Conferences, 3-5 June 2021, hosted online by UKEY Consulting and Publishing, London, United Kingdom

books, journals and conference proceedings to add appropriate significance to the study. Percentage method was administered to analyse both demographic characteristics of the study and perception of the respondents towards role and compensation related factors causing heavy workload. The result of the analysis has discovered that all the factors discussed in this study: complex organization structure; not communicating the objectives of the task and its importance towards organization to the sanitary workers; orientation and clear communication about work processes; lack of participation at departmental and organizational level decision making; frequent changes made in the organization and inadequate information about them; inadequate welfare facilities for sanitary workers; autocratic leadership style with lack of motivation; inadequate respect for sanitary workers and huge discrimination; and low and unfair salary system; discrimination in salary and other benefits were strongly agreed by majority of the respondents. The study has given suitable suggestions as to how to rationalize the organization structure and management practice related related factors causing heavy workload.

Keywords: Organization structure, management practice, heavy workload, sanitary worker, multi-speciality hospital, Tirunelveli city.

Forensic analysis of the Impact of covid-19 pandemic on the South African Economy

Benedict Ebenezer Alechenu
Technical University Kosice
Benedict.ebenezer.alechenu@tuke.sk

Abstract

The World economic activities were brought to a standstill in late 2019 through 2020 without a single gunshot but caused by a global pandemic called "Covid-19". Sadly, the root causes or origin of this pandemic is yet unknown despite all efforts by the World Health Organisation and other relevant authorities. Covid-19 has caused an unquantifiable economic damage more than expected in South Africa. It affected all facets of its economic system ranging from stock market, tourism industry, production industry e-tal. Global demand for South African export products fell by 14% of its GDP in the Q2 of 2020. Most major economies in the World lost more than 4% of their gross domestic product in 2020 and many countries entered recession due to the covid-19 pandemic. This pandemic has caused both hyperinflation and high rate of unemployment in South Africa. Data from 1960 shows that the second quarter of 2020 experienced a greater fall in GDP than the annualised decline of 6.1% in the first quarter of 2009 during the global financial crisis and was "far steeper than the annualised 8.2%

London International Conferences, 3-5 June 2021, hosted online by UKEY Consulting and Publishing, London, United Kingdom

decline in the fourth quarter of 1982". Overall, South African economy is still bedevilling/suffering from the collateral damages caused by covid-19 pandemic.

Keywords: Covid-19 pandemic, lockdown, Economy

1. Introduction

South African government imposed its first and one of the strictest lockdowns in the World to curtail the spread of covid-19 on the 27th of March 2020 and it was very successful. However, it took a heavy toll on the economy; because prior to the outbreak of the covid-19 pandemic, the economy was already in a technical recession. The hard lockdown imposed by the government added more salt to the already injured (fragile) economy. The imposed strict restrictions only allowed certain essential sectors to operate, forced small and medium businesses to endure greater strain on their operations, limited social gatherings and urged mask wearing and social distancing as part of the personal protective measures to minimise the spread of the virus.

1.1. Collateral Damages caused by Covid-19 pandemic on South African Economy

1. South African economy contracted for the first time in 11 years in 2020 as coronavirus lockdowns impeded/hindered the economy by disrupting trade and output.

2. Gross domestic product shrank by 7%, compared with a 0.2% expansion in 2019, according to a report released by Statistics South Africa.

3. Agriculture is the main driver on the economic growth, but contracted by 1.4%

4. Unemployment skyrocketed to all time high of 29%

5. Budget deficit widened to 4.5% caused by revenue shortfalls because of inactive commercial activities.

6. Those hit especially hard are already-impoverished female-headed households, those persons with only primary education, persons without social assistance, black populations, and heads of households who have been pushed from permanent to informal employment.

London International Conferences, 3-5 June 2021, hosted online by UKEY Consulting and Publishing, London, United Kingdom

2. Background of Study

2.1 Timeline of Government Actions on Covid-19 Pandemic in South Africa

First wave (March 2020-November 2020) = On the 5th of March 2020, South African Minister of health confirmed that a 38-year-old man from KwaZulu-Natal tested positive for Covid-19 shortly after returning from a trip to Italy. The patient and his close contacts were placed in isolation and monitored by health officials. The first death to have occurred from the disease was reported on 27 March 2020.

On the 15th of March 2020, the government announced the first quarantine location for South Africans returning from abroad at "The Ranch Resort in Polokwane" shortly after that, President, Ramaphosa announced the 21-day lockdown in South Africa from 26 March to 16 April 2020 with the hope of reducing/minimising the spread of the virus.

From 1st May 2020, a gradual and phased easing of the lockdown restrictions began, lowering the national alert level from level 5 to level 4. On the 1st of June 2020, it was eased to level 3. On the 15th of August President Ramaphosa announced that after the passing of the COVID-19 peak, the lockdown will be lowered to level 2. On 21 September, lockdown was finally eased to level 1.

Second wave (December 2020-present) = After the discovery of the *B.1.351 lineage*, also known as *20H/501Y.V2* (formerly 20C/501Y.V2), *501Y.V2 variant*, and colloquially known as *South African COVID-19 variant* on 18 December 2020, and the rise of cases after surpassing 1 million people tested positive, it was announced on 28 December that the country would go back to a partial lockdown level 3 to reduce the spread of the second wave during the festive season.

The national vaccination program in South Africa was set to begin in early February 2021, after receiving its 1st 1,000,000 doses of Oxford-AstraZeneca vaccine, but on the 7th of February, South African Health Products Regulatory Authority (SAPHRA) suspended the vaccine after it proved to be ineffective against the 501.V2 variant.

On the 17th of February 2021, the national Covid vaccination program was officially rolled out after receiving its first 80,000 doses of the Johnson & Johnson vaccine. On the 17th of March 2021, South African Health Products Regulatory Authority (SAHPRA) has approved Pfizer/BioNTech for use.

Today 01-06-2021, South Africa has recorded over 1.669,231million confirmed Covid-19 cases, 42,895 active confirmed cases, 1,546,558million recoveries and over 56,601deaths.

3. Methodology Applied

Secondary data from multiple sources such as published articles, unpublished articles, Newspapers etc, were used to conduct this forensic analysis of the impact of Covid-19 pandemic on the South African Economy. Data from Twelve most infected African countries were collected for a comparative analysis. This will help us to know the collateral damages caused by covid-19 on both human and material resources on South Africa and its huge economic impacts.

Table:1 Table of actual cases in 12 most affected African countries (as of 27 May 2021)

Country	Confirmed	Active	Recoveries	Deaths

	cases	confirmed cases		
South Africa	1,645,555	42,895	1,546,583	56,170
Morocco	518,122	2,780	506,208	9,134
Tunisia	338,853	27,600	298,855	12,398
Ethiopia	270,527	31,974	234,426	4,127
Egypt	257,275	53,858	188,567	14,850
Libya	184,472	10,351	171,006	3,115
Kenya	169,697	50,601	115,988	3,108
Nigeria	166,146	7,546	156,529	2,071
Algeria	127,926	35,438	89,040	3,448
Ghana	93,711	1,211	91,707	783
Zambia	93,627	1,115	91,239	1,273
Cameroon	77,982	3,786	72,926	1,270

Source:
https://en.wikipedia.org/wiki/Template:COVID19_pandemic_data/South_A
fricamedical_cases_chart

Table:2 Daily Covid-19 Cases in South Africa from 13-05-2021-01-06-2021

Date	Confirmed cases	Deaths
2021-05-13	1,605,252	55,012
2021-05-14	1,608,393(+0.2)	55,124(+0.2%)
2021-05-15	1,611,143(+0.17%)	55,183(+0.11%)
2021-05-16	1,613,728(+0.16%)	55,210(+0.05%)
2021-05-17	1,615,485(+0.11%)	55,260(+0.09%)
2021-05-18	1,617,840(+0.15%)	55,340(+0.14%)
2021-05-19	1,621,362(+0.22%)	55,507(+0.3%)
2021-05-20	1,625,003(+0.22%)	55,568(+0.11%)
2021-05-21	1,628,335(+0.21%)	55,719(+0.27%)
2021-05-22	1,632,572(+0.26%)	55,772(+0.1%)
2021-05-23	1,635,465(+0.18%)	55,802(+0.05%)
2021-05-24	1,637,848(+0.15%)	55,874(+0.13%)
2021-05-25	1,640,932(+0.19%)	55,976(+0.18%)
2021-05-26	1,645,555(+0.27%)	55,077(+0.18%)
2021-05-27	1,649,977(+0.27%)	56,170(+0.17%)
2021-05-28	1,654,551(+0.28%)	56,293(+0.22%)
2021-05-29	1,659,070(+0.27%)	56,363(+0.12%)
2021-05-30	1,662,825(+0.23%)	56,439(+0.13%)
2021-05-31	1,665,617(+0.12)	56,506(+0.12%)
2021-06-01	1,669,231(+0.22)	56,601(+0.17%)

Sources:
1.https://en.wikipedia.org/wiki/Template:COVID19_pandemic_data/South_Africa_
medical_cases_chart

London International Conferences, 3-5 June 2021, hosted online by UKEY
Consulting and Publishing, London, United Kingdom

2. https://www.statista.com/statistics/1170463/coronavirus-cases-in-africa/

4. Data analysis and Results

Data collected were analysed and the results obtained were crucial to ascertain the impact of covid-19 on the South African Economy. Results obtained shows that South Africa has both the highest infection rates and death rates in Africa. Results were analysed using graphs for more accuracy and explanations.

Fig.1 A clustered column line chart showing actual cases of Covid-19 in 12most affected African countries as of 27th May 2021.

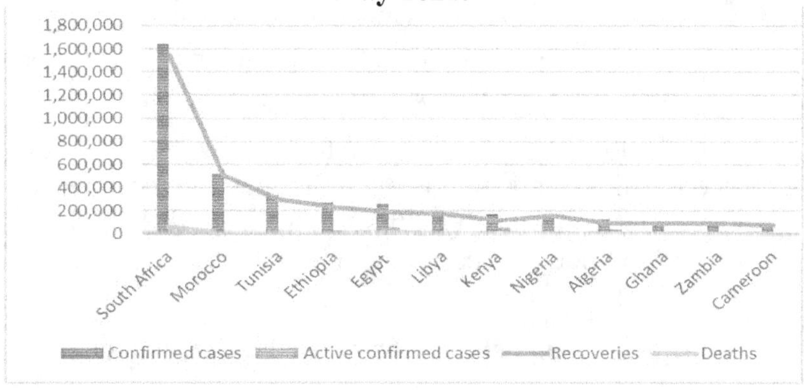

South Africa has both the highest confirmed cases and death on the continent of Africa.

Morocco has the second highest confirmed cases, while Egypt has the second highest death.

During the period under review, Cameroon has both the lowest confirmed cases sand death among the selected countries.

London International Conferences, 3-5 June 2021, hosted online by UKEY Consulting and Publishing, London, United Kingdom

Surprisingly, Nigeria the most populous country on the continent was not badly hit both confirmed cases and deaths.

5. Conclusion

The impact of Covid-19 on South African economy is undoubtedly huge and the quick response by the government got a mixed reaction from the people. The government was caught in the crossroads between the decision to save lives versus livelihoods but opted for saving lives. Hence the government imposed a strict lockdown to curtail the virus.

The Government's strong leadership and bold actions to contain the pandemic (including a total lockdown, implementation of a stimulus package, aggressive screening, and testing) were globally acknowledged; yet the COVID-19 remained untamed in the first five months – with devastating impacts on the economy and the population.

The loss of lives in South Africa due to covid-19 has left an indelible mark on both their families and the country in general. As at 02-06-2021, 56,601 people have died of Covid-19 in South Africa, while the total deaths in Africa stood at 131,317.

Government debt has increased drastically in double fold.

According to SA statistics, GDP shrank 7%, compared with a 0.2% expansion in 2019.

Private businesses were the hardest hit. To cushion the effect of the lockdown, the government borrowed money to pay unemployment benefits which has brought a heavy debt burden on the economy (weak RAN)

Unemployment rate skyrocketed and inflation rate is in double digits as a result of Covid-19 pandemic.

London International Conferences, 3-5 June 2021, hosted online by UKEY Consulting and Publishing, London, United Kingdom

Bibliography

Africanews.com (2021). Covid-19 shrinks South Africa's economy
for first time in 11 years.
https://www.africanews.com/2021/03/09/covid-19-shrinks-
south-africa-s-economy-for-first-time-in-11-years

Arnt, C; Robinson, S. (2020). Who has been hit hardest by South
Africa's lockdown? We found some answers.
https://theconversation.com/who-has-been-hit-hardest-by-
south-africas-lockdown-we-found-some-answers-138481.
https://www.ifpri.org/publication/who-has-been-hit-hardest-
south-africaslockdown-we-found-some-answers.

Arnt, C; Davies, R; Gabriel, S; Harris, L; Makrelov, K; Robinson, S;
Anderson, L. (2020).

Covid-19 lockdowns, income distribution, and food security: An
analysis for South Africa.
https://www.ifpri.org/publication/covid-19-lockdowns-
income-distribution-and-food-security-analysis-south-africa

Arnt, C; Davies, R; Gabriel, S; Harris, L; Makrelov, K; Robinson,S;
Anderson, L; Modise, B Simbanegavi, W; Seventer, D, V.
(2020). Impact of covid-19 on the South African Economy
Working paper. https://www.ifpri.org/publication/impact-
covid-19- south-african-economy-initial-analysis

Galal, F. (2021). Corona Deaths in Africa.
https://www.statista.com/statistics/1170530/coronavirus-
deaths-in-africa/

Naidu, S. (2021). The Impact of covid-19: The conundrum of South
Africa's Socio-Economy Landscape.
https://www.accord.org.za/analysis/the-impact-of-covid-19-
the-conundrum-of-south-africas-socio-economic-landscape/

Trading Economics (2021). Coronavirus Covid-19 cases by Country.
https://tradingeconomics.com/country-list/coronavirus-cases

United Nations Development programme (2020). Covid-19 in South
Africa: Socio- Economic Impact Assessment.
https://reliefweb.int/sites/reliefweb.int/files/resources/UNDP

Wikipedia (2021). COVID-19 pandemic data/South Africa medical
        cases chart https://en.wikipedia.org/wiki/Template:COVID-
        19_pandemic_data/South_Africamedical_cases_chart

World meters (2021). Reported Cases and Deaths by Country or
        Territory. https://www.worldometers.info/coronavirus

CONSULTING & PUBLISHING

London International Conferences

londonic.uk

ukeyconsultingpublishing.co.uk

National Strategy to Combat Covid 19

Bambang Sugiyono Agus Purwono
State Polytechnic of Malang, Indonesia
https://orcid.org/0000-0001-8515-1868
bambang.sugiyono@polinema.ac.id

M. Fahim Tharaba
Universitas Islam Negeri Maulana
Malik Ibrahim, Malang

Shyamala Susan
APC Mahalaxmi College for
Women, Thoothukudi, Tamilnadu,
India

Ali Nasith
Universitas Islam Negeri Maulana
Malik Ibrahim, Malang Indonesia

M. Jasin
Universitas Islam Negeri Syarif
Hidayatulah, Jakarta, Indonesia

Abstract

The aims of this paper is to design the National (Indonesia) Strategic Planning to combat Covid 19. The research method is qualitative (or subjective) approach using secondary data. The research results are eight steps to design Strategic Planning to combat Covid 19. There are Vision, Mission, Objectives, Strategy, Policy, Program, Budgets, and Procedures. The Vision of strategic planning is National (Indonesia) Strategy to End COVID-19 in 2022. And the Strategy is National (Indonesia) Strategy to Combat COVID-19 in 2022.

Keywords: Strategic Planning, combat, Covid 19, Vision, Strategy.

London International Conferences, 3-5 June 2021, hosted online by UKEY Consulting and Publishing, London, United Kingdom

B. S. Agus Purwono
M. F. Tharaba, S. Susan
A. Nasith, M. Jasin

1. Introduction

The President (Republic of Indonesia) Joko "Jokowi" Widodo finally declared a COVID-19 public health emergency on March 31, one month after the first two cases in the country were confirmed on March 2, 2020.

The President issued Government Regulation No. 21/2020 on large-scale social distancing as an implementing regulation of the 2018 Health Quarantine Law to restrict the movement of people and goods within a control zone but he stopped short of allowing regional administrations to close their borders.

The President has also decided not to ban the "mudik" (mass exodus) on Ied (Idul Fitri), although he has advised people not to "mudik." [1].

1.1. Large-scale social restrictions (3), include [1]:

1. The closure of schools and workplaces.

2. Restrictions on religious activities.
3. Restrictions on activities in public places.

1.2. The large-scale social restrictions stipulated in the Health Quarantine Law, namely:

1. Home quarantine.

2. Hospital quarantine.
3. Regional quarantine.

2. Literature study
2.1.   The Eight steps designing the Strategic Planning [2]

Figure 1 shows that there are the eight (8) steps designing the Strategic Planning, include: Vision, Mission, Objectives, Strategy, Policy, Program, Budgets, and Procedures.

B. S. Agus Purwono
M. F. Tharaba, S. Susan
A. Nasith, M. Jasin

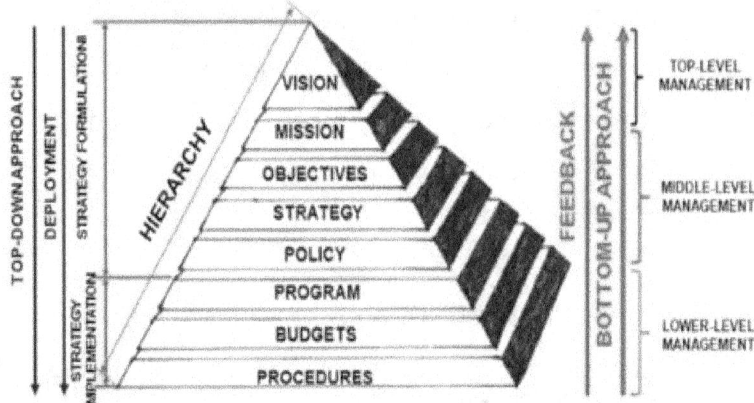

Figure 1. The Eight steps designing the Strategic Planning [2]

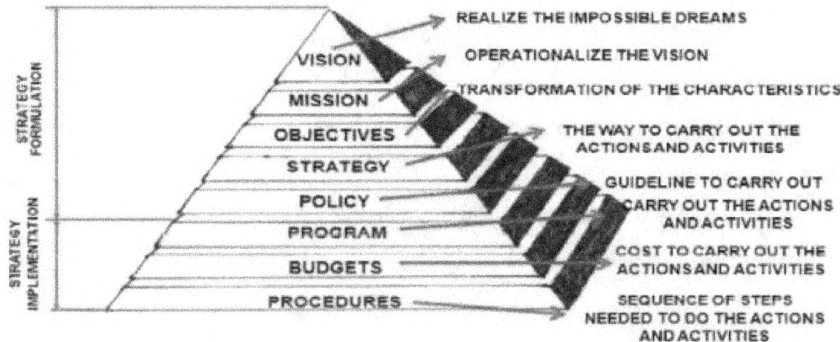

Figure 2. The definition of each steps in the Strategic Planning [2]

2.2. The definition of each steps in the Strategic Planning

Vision is to realize the impossible dreams.

Mission is to operationalize the vision.

Objectives is to transform the characteristics.

Strategy is the way to carry out the actions and activities.

B. S. Agus Purwono
M. F. Tharaba, S. Susan
A. Nasith, M. Jasin

Policy is the guidelines to carry out the actions and activities.

Program is to carry out the actions and activities.

Budgets is the cost to carry out the actions and activities.

Procedures is the sequence of steps needed to do the actions and activities.

3. Results and discussion

The operationale of **National Strategy Planning to Combat COVID 19 are:**

Vision: National (Indonesia) Strategy to End COVID-19 in 2022.

Mission: Everyone participate in reducing the number by practicing the "3M" health protocols:

1. Mask wearing
2. Hand washing
3. Social/physical distancing

Objectives:

1. To issued the task force to responsible and to socialize the pandemic of suspected COVID-19.
2. To curb the spead of the virus COVID-19 quickly, or decrease the mortality, or to reduce and eliminate the number of suspected COVID-19.
3. To help the country achieve herd immunity faster, or to prepare the vaccin till 460 million doses, or to innoculate 181.5 million people on March 2022 with priority.

Strategy: National (Indonesia) Strategy to Combat COVID-19 in 2022.

B. S. Agus Purwono
M. F. Tharaba, S. Susan
A. Nasith, M. Jasin

Policy:

1. To prepare for if the situation gets significantly worse.

2. The President has issued Government Regulation (UU) No. 23/2020 on Large-Scale Social Distancing; Large-Scale Social restrictions, include:

a. The closure of schools and workplaces
b. Restriction on religious activities
c.   Restriction on activities in public places
d. Restrictions stipulated in the Health Quarantine Law, namely:
-   Home quarantine
-   Hospital quarantine
-   Regional quarantine

3. The government has issued Government Regulation (UU) No. 23/1959, implies a heavy – handed security approach

4. President has also decided not to ban the "mudik" (mass exodus) on Ied (Idul Fitri) although he has advised people not to "mudik."

Program: "Iman, Aman, and Imun."

"Iman" means faith, "aman" means safety, referring to the 3M health protocols, and "imun" means to encourage people to improve their immunity system."
Budgets:

The government has issued PERPPU (Government Regulation Lieu of Law) No. 1/2020 on State Financial Policy and Financial System Stability, refocusing state expenditure of Rp. 405.1 trillion (USD 19 billion) on:

1. The health sector
2. Social-welfare safety net

3. Tax incentive.

London International Conferences, 3-5 June 2021, hosted online by UKEY Consulting and Publishing, London, United Kingdom

4. Conclusion:

The conclusions of this paper are:

1. There are eight steps to design Strategic Planning to combat Covid 19 include: Vision, Mission, Objectives, Strategy, Policy, Program, Budgets, and Procedures.
2. The Vision is National (Indonesia) Strategy to End COVID-19 in 2022.
3. The Strategy is National (Indonesia) Strategy to Combat COVID-19 in 2022.

B. S. Agus Purwono
M. F. Tharaba, S. Susan
A. Nasith, M. Jasin

References:

[1] https://www.thejakartapost.com/news/2020/04/03/indonesias-strategy-to-combat-covid-19-what-we-know-so-far.html. Accesed April 4, 2021.

[2] Purwono, Bambang Sugiyono Agus Purwono, et al. 2013. National Renewable Energy Strategy. Elsevier. Energy Procedia. Volume 23 (2013), pp. 136-144.

[3] https://www.thejakartapost.com/news/2020/10/03/bkkbn-to-assist-covid-19-task-force-in-socializing-3m-health-protocols.html. Accessed April 1, 2021.

[4] Supriatna, Encup. 2020. Socio-Economic Impacts of The COVID-19 Pandemic: The Case of Bandung City. Journal of Governance Volume 5, Issue 1, June 2020. Pp. 61-70. P-ISSN 2528-276X; E-ISSN 2598-6465. http://dx.doi.org/10.31506/jog.v5i1.8041

[5] Mufida, Saleha, F.G. Cempaka Timur, Surryanto Djoko Waluyo. 2020. Strategi Pemerintah Indonesia Dalam Menangani Wabah Covid-19 Dari Perspektif Ekonomi. Volume 1 No.2. Oktober 2020. e-ISSN : 2721-9755

London International Conferences

londonic.uk   ukeyconsultingpublishing.co.uk

Digital? Local? Transparent? – Six truths of supply chains after Covid-19

Christina Schabasser
University of Applied Sciences Burgenland
christina.schabasser@live.at

Abstract

Supply chains were and always will be exposed to risks. The increasing complexity of today´s supply chains pose the greatest challenges to supply chain management. Disruptions of the supply chain caused by disasters (e.g., the Covid-19 pandemic) indicates that the inter-organizational interaction between purchasing, production and logistics on a mostly global level does not work as smoothly as assumed. Although, there were serious disasters with dire effects on global supply chains even before Covid-19, supply chains have hardly lost any of their complexity or gained in transparency. Therefore, it is important to address this issue with the utmost urgency to make supply chains more resilient. The article aims to answer the question how the supply chains of the future could look like. Six levers for restructuring or redesigning supply chains are presented in this paper, for example, higher safety stocks and a diversified supplier portfolio. Even if the supply chains known to us will not cease to exist, current practices will certainly be reassessed. A conceptual model and its visualization opportunities is used to illustrate how a supply chain is skipped out of balance. It forces the reader to think about solutions to stabilize supply chains, resulting in a new (extended or deeper) understanding of phenomena for interested people, supply chain managers, practitioners, and researchers in this field.

Keywords: Supply chain disruption, Covid-19 pandemic, conceptual model.

London International Conferences, 3-5 June 2021, hosted online by UKEY Consulting and Publishing, London, United Kingdom

1. Introduction

Worldwide, the manufacturing processes are divided into different phases and carried out in different parts of the world, which are often far away from the consumer of the finished products. Supply chains around the world are stimulated by the idea of cost optimization, cost-cutting, and just-in-time production. Holding excessive inventories is often seen as a sign of waste (Javorcik, 2020). The growth of global supply chains resulted in an increasing specialization of companies in certain activities and phases in supply chains instead of taking care of all the subtasks. The huge importance of (global) supply chains is evidenced by the fact that over 70% of global trade results from intermediate goods and services and capital goods (OECD, WTO, World Bank Group, 2014). Nowadays, there is an ever-decreasing vertical range of manufacture. In return, this means that company's hand over responsibility, as fewer services are produced from in-house production.

The more complex and therefore intertwined and international the nature of supply chains, the more vulnerable they are to risks such as natural disasters, strikes and terrorism (Bundschuh, 2003). There seems to be a causal relationship between the complexity of the supply chain and the severity of an interruption. There is no such thing as a risk-free supply chain, therefore, supply chain disruptions are unavoidable; but some supply chain disruptions are more serious than others, which has to do with the complexity of a supply chain (Blackhurst et al, 2005). The growing number of disasters over the past decades should be enough reason to reflect on how resilient supply chains can be achieved in future. Figure 1 shows the exponential growth in natural and man-made (e.g., terrorist attacks) disasters over the years.

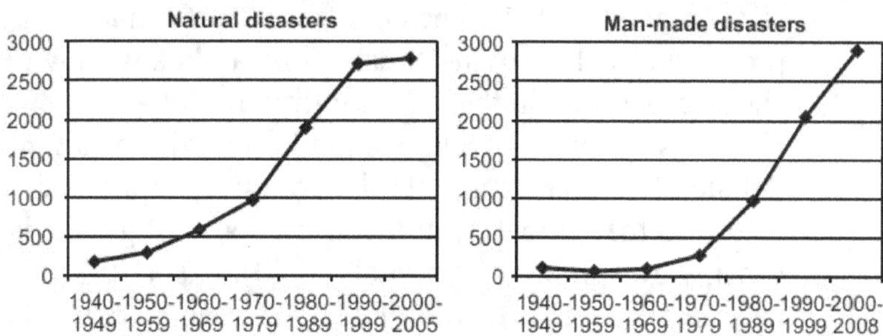

Figure 1. Distribution of natural and man-made disasters from 1940 to 2005

Source: Centre for Research on the Epidemiology of Disasters, 2004

Just-in-time (JIT) production, which is standardized in many industries, assumes that the supply chains always perform exactly as planned. Although, JIT is not a panacea to unplanned changes in the requirements that will be transmitted to the entire supply chain. JIT can be a successful concept in case of stable and predictable demand, but disastrous when everyone in the supply chain is only familiar with a certain part of production and therefore cannot take care of problem solving themselves in the event of a failure (Nahmias et al., 2015). As companies' supply chains become more complex and distributed, it becomes more difficult to establish transparent supply chains, but transparency in the supply chains would be important so that companies can understand them and reduce the inherent risk potential. If a company does not know which suppliers are in its supply chain and then the supply chain of a company is interrupted, it can at least react and replenish the supply or replace the supplier. When this response is not possible due to a lack of transparency, the brand reputation of the company which is affected by the disruption in the supply chain suffers. Different stakeholder groups call for better visualization of suppliers and the flow of inputs, goods and services in a given supply chain

London International Conferences, 3-5 June 2021, hosted online by UKEY Consulting and Publishing, London, United Kingdom

(Kashmanian, 2017). The collapse in performance in China provoked by the Covid-19 pandemic and its worldwide impact showed once again the vulnerability of global supply chains. Whereas the end of globalization will hardly be a topic for debate, it is important to think about the supply chains of the future so that global manufacturing does not get further into a downward spiral (Holger et al., 2020). A survey from 2020 carried out by the Austrian Federal Economic Chamber provides information about the resilience of supplier networks of Austrian companies. It is worth mentioning that the questionnaires had to be submitted by mid-April 2020, in the middle of the Covid-19 pandemic. The study has shown how dependent Austrian companies of all sizes are on their suppliers and what disastrous consequences this has. Alarmingly, more than a third (1/3) of the companies surveyed stated that they had at least one supplier whose failure would lead to a complete business breakdown (Complexity Science Hub, 2020). Do resilient supply chains have a lot to do with fantasy and little to do with reality? The limitation or failure of production due to the lack of preliminary products caused by the Covid-19 pandemic gives rise to doubts about the international division of labor. Companies are strongly integrated into international supply chains when their products are based on inputs from specialized suppliers from all over the world (Bunde, 2021). The result for companies that focus too much on cost efficiency and less on security of supply becomes dramatically clear in the event of a collapse (Bogaschewsky, 2020).

Within the present work, the terms value chain and supply chain are understood as synonyms. There is no hard line to distinguish between supply chains and value chains. The difference could be determined by the fact that in supply chain relationships, one looks at the import of intermediate inputs and in the value chain one looks at the import of added value. Take the (fictive) example of VW Wolfsburg that imports automobile wheels from Poland, consisting of rims and car tires worth 100 euros each, Steel and light metal come from China (40 euros), valves from South Korea (10 euros), car tires from Japan (30 euros), the value of the assembly in Poland (20 euros). When looking at the intermediate inputs it can be stated that Germany imports inputs worth 100 euros from Poland (and it is completely dependent on Poland for car wheel deliveries). Considering the value-added imports, one can say that Germany imports value added worth 20 euros from Poland and the rest from the other countries mentioned. Here it becomes clear that Germany is depending on several countries for the supply of automobile wheels. If all of this can be assembled in Germany without major additional costs, one would not have to rely on imports from Poland at all, but only on imports from China, South Korea, and Japan (Petersen, T., email communication, May 16th, 2021).

2. Literature
2.1. Managing supply chain complexity

Before starting a more in-depth discussion, it makes sense to demonstrate the complexity of a supply chain. A complete supply chain can be imagined as a connection between nodes

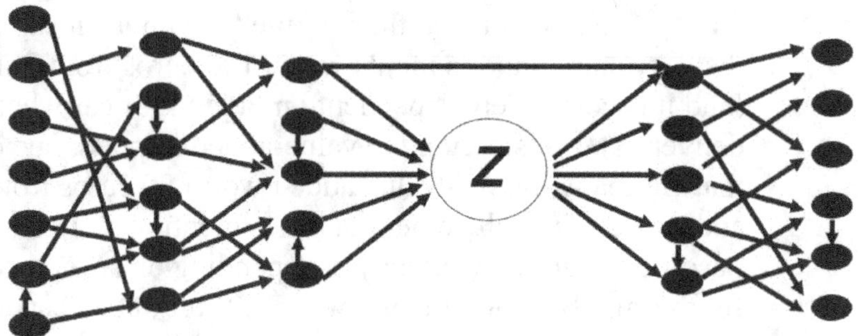

(organizational units) and arcs (all internodal relationships between the place of origin and the place of end use). The supply chain of manufacturer Z (see fig.2) includes different entities (i.e., firms) which are linked by a physical flow of materials. If one imagines that manufacturer Z replaces a supplier with a poor performance by another, then this leads to a restructuring of the essence of the supply chain itself (Blackhurst et al., 2005).

Figure 2: Supply chain structure for manufacturer Z

Source: Blackhurst et al., 2005

There are various forms of complexity in a supply chain, on the one hand, there is the static complexity that describes the connectivity and structure of the subsystems contributing to the supply chain (e.g., companies, business functions and processes). It is important to keep an eye on not only the structural but also the dynamic complexity stemming from the operating behavior of the system and its environment that addresses the factors time and randomness. Finally, there is also the complexity of decision-making, which includes elements of both structural and dynamic complexity, the inherent complexity in supply chain makes it difficult to manage them and therefore it is by no means inconsequential to claim that supply chain management is about managing the complexity of the supply chains. A supply chain complexity driver is any characteristic of a supply chain that heightens the supply chain complexity. Examples of static complexity drivers are number /variety of products and processes. Process uncertainties is an example of dynamic complexity. The decision as to whether a supply chain should be managed by a centralized or decentralized decision making or to what extent decision-making is automated, is part of the decision-making complexity (SerdarAsan, 2013).

2.2. Redundancy: a source of resilience

Sheffi et al. (2005) assume that the resilience of a supply chain, i.e., how quickly a supply chain is functional again after a disruption, can be achieved through redundancy or flexibility. Redundancy can be generated by multiple sourcing or safety stock. Additional suppliers as well as safety stocks are associated with costs, but this cost of redundancy should be seen as a sort of insurance premium.

2.2.1. Multiple Sourcing

At the latest after the outbreak of the Covid-19 pandemic, the word "redundancy" found its way into the supply chain vocabulary. Robustness or resilience of supply chains require redundancy in suppliers. The so-called supplier diversification can strengthen the "immune system" of the supply chain. If one supplier fails, another one can jump in and fix the problem. This would be one of the advantages of a diversified supplier base. On the other hand, one must also consider that a less diversified pool of suppliers can also be advantageous. the higher purchasing volumes at concentrated supplier base also give buyers the opportunity to make investments that ensure a rapid recovery of the supply chain in the event of a disruption. Does the sourcing from many different suppliers enable faster recovery in the event of a disruption? Further influencing factors could also be the depth of the relationship to the suppliers (Jain et al., 2020). Berger et al 2004 investigate the question of whether one should opt for a single or multiple sourcing strategy from the point of view of risk management. The question is how high the number of suppliers should be to guarantee the functionality of the supply chain even in the event of a catastrophe? The authors present a decision-tree base on optimization model to evaluate both procurement strategies and differentiate between so-called "super-events" that affect all suppliers at the same time and so-called "unique-events" that only affect a specific supplier in the supply chain and calculate the probabilities for the occurrence of such "events". They find that the number of suppliers stays stable when the risk of super-events affecting suppliers is low. It also found that the optimal number of suppliers increases when the risk of events affecting suppliers increases significantly (Berger et al., 2004). According to the Institute for Supply Chain Management, the responses from companies to the Covid-19 pandemic suggest that much more attention is paid to the supply base and that risk diversification is sought by qualifying alternative and / or additional suppliers (Institute for Supply Management).

2.2.2. Safety Stocks

Since redundancy is to be understood in such a way that resources are kept in reserve for the event of a fault, safety stocks, besides the use of multiple suppliers, are also a common form of the redundancy concept (Sheffi et al., 2005). Although the JIT principle undoubtedly has its advantages, it is designed for nominal operation and not for interruptions. In the future, companies will concentrate more on ensuring operational continuity than on the issues of waste and inefficiencies. That would mean that in the future, companies would keep enough inventories to counter uncertainties in supply and demand. The issues of efficiency, flexibility, resilience, and reliability have no longer be trade-off. "Just in Case" means that companies create contingency plans for crisis scenarios and agree on higher procurement costs, accept longer times of delivery, and put more emphasis on reliability than on cost-effectiveness when selecting suppliers (Fonseca et al., 2020). Relatively at the beginning of the Covid-19 pandemic, it was already apparent how quickly efficient, cost-effective just-in-time production can develop into a cost-intensive, high-risk strategy. To be better prepared to global shocks like Covid-19 in the future, companies will probably have to reduce their dependence on global production chains and intermediate deliveries by holding larger inventories or buffers at or near their production location (Brakman et al., 2020).

2.3. Flexibility: an important resilience factor

Flexibility can be seen as the lever for resilient supply chains, if one realizes once again that the resilience of a supply chain can be generated through redundancy and flexibility, then one certainly has more opportunity to generate resilience by pressing the "flexibility lever". In a supply chain, the material flow from the supplier takes place through a conversion process as well as distribution channels and is governed by various systems that all work in terms of the corporate culture. Each of the five elements supply, conversion, distribution, control systems and corporate culture gives room for flexibility.

2.4. IT and digitization

The complexity of today´s supply chains would probably not function without information technology and digitization. There are several advantages that IT and digitization create for supply chains. Examples include the reduction in cycle time, higher efficiency, higher performance and the traceability and visibility of the product flow. Despite these advantages that IT and digitization offer for supply chains, doubts can arise, especially in times of major disruptions such as the corona pandemic. (Gupta et al., 2020).

Table 1 gives an overview of main digitization tools used in Supply Chain management.

Table 1: Ground-breaking technologies in supply chains

Technology	Explanation of technology	Advantages through technology
Big data analytics, (Gupta et al., 2020)	The components of Big Data Analytics include predictive analytics, statistical analysis, and data mining.	The technology can lead to increased business profits and increases in efficiency.
Internet of Things (IoT), (Ben-Daya et al., 2019)	Intelligent objects communicate with their environment; the data they emit provide useful insight into all aspects of the supply chain.	IoT speeds up the time between data collection and decision making,
Blockchain Technology (Kim et al., 2018)	The promising Blockchain technologies can be seen as a decentralized database that provides highly secure and well-protected access to supply chain data.	Blockchain Technology can be a confidence-building measure within a supply chain.

Source: own representation

The Covid-19 pandemic raises the question of whether digitization turns out to be a false promise. The integration of artificial intelligence (AI) into digital processes has been largely assessed as progress, but the Covid-19 pandemic revealed deficits of AI, because the algorithms are fragile to extreme and ahistorical events. Inventory management systems that otherwise do a good job by predicting production rates and consumer demand have failed in the Covid-19 pandemic. AI-algorithm-supported digitization works reasonably well under "normal" circumstances due to its ability to self-correct and adapt to ordinary pattern changes. However, the pandemic made it necessary for humans to intervene in the highly digitized processes. The human with his expertise was needed to find out the causes and effects of sudden shifts in consumer demand patterns or to identify the impacts of the lockdown on the continuation of the supply chain and transport. The necessity of human expertise and judgement became apparent. It should not be forgotten that the systems are immensely powerful and often process exceptionally large amounts of data, but they have a naive worldview (Faraj et al., 2021).

2.5. Rising regionalism

The Covid-19 pandemic clearly demonstrates the weaknesses of globalization, the logical consequence arises from this could be a return to more regionalism. But it remains to be seen whether supply chains will become more local in the future. Even though voices are raised for more regionalization in supply chains, it is important to emphasize not only the strong points but also the weaknesses of more regional supply chains. The decline in global supply chains would have negative effects on the economic development of emerging and developing countries, especially from Southeast Asian. Countries that are currently not yet integrated into global supply chains (e.g., some countries in Africa) would have a harder time achieving this integration (Görg et al., 2020). According to a McKinsey study conducted in May 2020, 93% of the supply chain executives surveyed want to make their supply chains more resilient in the future, they want to achieve this, among other things, by regionalizing the supply chains (McKinsey Global Institute, 2020). If one were to turn one´s back on hyper-globalization, then advantages such as high growth rates, reduced poverty and opportunities for less qualified workers would also be lost. The cost of regionalizing supply chains should not be underestimated, especially in places where support services are lacking and there are no efficient transport and communication links. To what extent regionalization of the supply chains will take place also depends on the industry.

2.6. Product variety – but not at all costs

Today´s supply chains face a trade-off between product variety and supply chain performance. The dramatic increase in product variety in most industries does not stop at supply chains either. Many companies have misjudged the costs of a high variety of products and therefore keep a higher variety of products than would be good for them.

3. Research Methodology

The research objective of this study is to analyze the existing literature on supply chain disruption and to uncover six key truths about resilient and more resilient supply chains for the future. The study also tries to create awareness for supply chain managers at which points in the supply chain an adjustment leads to less complexity, for example. An expert interview with Prof. Dr. Rainer Thiele from IFW Kiel Institut für Weltwirtschaft shows how the trends are understood from the perspective of an expert.

Visualization of connections and causal dependencies can create transparency. Therefore, the situation of an economic downturn is visualized in a small conceptual model.

3.1. Design

An attempt is made to create a conceptual model on supply chain disruption using the Garp3 workbench. The models of cause-and-effect relationships implemented in Garp3

(Bredeweg et al., 2009) attempt to make the complexity of a corporate crisis manageable. The adequate formalization of the domain-specific knowledge not only creates transparency, understanding and traceability for decision-makers in supply chain management, but also for researchers in the field of complexity and crisis management.

3.2. Sample

The Covid-19 pandemic has brought the topic "supply chain disruptions" back into the economic headlines. To create the starting point for the article, current economic newspapers, articles, and online reports on the effects of Covid-19 on supply chains were searched vigorously. So, a high practical relevance was in the foreground when deriving the 6 truths about the supply chains of the future (see fig. 3).

In addition, the economic literature was researched to check whether these six truths conform to the unanimous opinion and, where it was not so, to open a discussion.

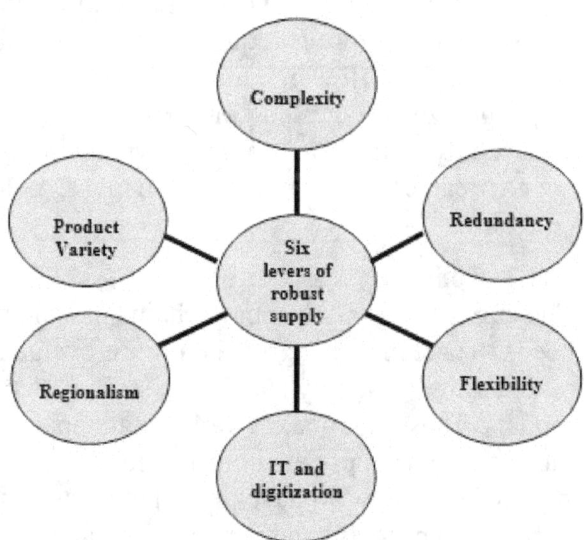

Figure 3: Six levers of robust supply chains

Source: own representation

3.3. Procedure
3.3.1. Expert opinion

Now the most important insights form the expert interview are summarized (Thiele, R., telephone interview, May 26th, 2021).

- The supply chains have become a bit shorter in general, but not only because of Covid-19.
- It may depend more on the branch of industry if supply chains will change or not.
- For example, a major technical change is taking place in the automotive supply chain (e.g. switching to e-cars), but this has nothing to do with Covid-19.
- Supply chains could change because a re-orientation in terms of China may take place.
- A step towards multiple sourcing will probably take place, but not only because of Covid-19.
- A regionalization of the supply chains will probably happen, but the stronger ones will prevail.
- Political cooperation also shows how little one can rely on, but structure is required for supply chains to work.
- Managers will weigh more risks and consider how to organize products and processes.
- Supply chains for booking travel and long-distance trips to African countries will be permanently affected by Covid-19.

3.3.2. Conceptual model

The current fate of the supply chains has shown that a rethink needs to take place. A great help in re-evaluating current practices in the supply chain is to work with conceptual models. These can make visible what happens, for example, in the event of a supply chain disruption, i.e., what influences such a disruption can have and what measures could be taken to restore a peaceful and functioning balance in the supply chain. The catchphrases here are probably "transparency through visualization" and "visualization as an opportunity".

To put it simply, one could imagine a trade-off between the complexity of a supply chain and its vulnerability, which can subsequently also be understood as a conflict between advantages and downsides. The more complex supply chains are, the more vulnerable they are. One of the reasons for the increasing complexity is that companies want to remain competitive and thus also want to produce more cost-effectively.

The basic assumption is that "vulnerability" follows the development of "drive". In the example, the stimulus arises from a worldwide Covid-19 pandemic and determines the level of vulnerability of supply chains.

The model fragment "The Covid-19 pandemic as a trigger for supply chains' vulnerability" (see Fig. 4) consists of the entities "Covid19 pandemic" and "Global supply chain x", the two quantities "drive" and "vulnerability" as well as the configuration "influences". "Drive" and "vulnerability" are characterized by the quantity space {zero, plus}. A positive direct influence ("I +") describes the causality between "drive" and "vulnerability". "I +" causes the following development of the quantities: if the current value of "Drive" is positive, the "vulnerability" increases; if "Drive" has the value 0, then "vulnerability" remains unchanged. Expectations are as follows: the assumption is that "vulnerability" follows the development of "drive".

London International Conferences, 3-5 June 2021, hosted online by UKEY Consulting and Publishing, London, United Kingdom

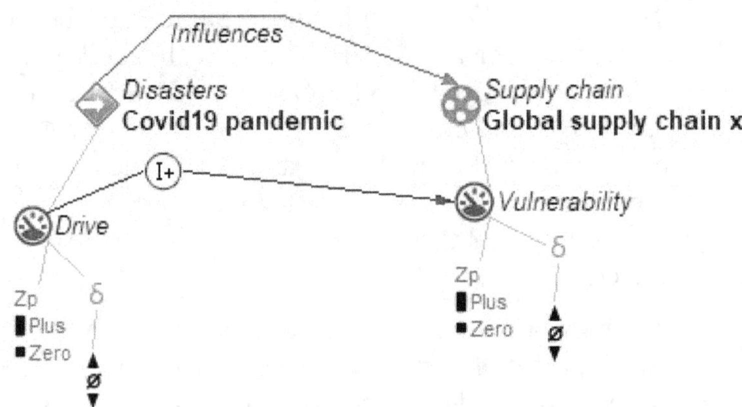

Figure 4: The Covid-19 pandemic as a trigger for supply chains´ vulnerability

Source: own representation

In the model fragment "Rebalancing the supply chain" (see Fig. 5) a mathematical calculation (minus) is used to determine the "complexity rate" from the difference between "vulnerability" and "complexity". The causal relationship between the quantities is described by a positive proportionality ("P +"), which leads from the quantity "vulnerability" to the quantity "complexity rate". "P +" means that the "complexity rate" increases when "vulnerability" increases, "complexity rate" decreases when "vulnerability" decreases and "complexity rate" remains the same when "vulnerability" remains the same. For the negative proportionality ("P-"), as it is used in the relationship between "complexity" and "complexity rate", exactly the opposite applies. A positive proportionality ("P +") is used to describe the causal relationship between the "complexity rate" and "diversification". The causality between "diversification" and "complexity" is described by a direct influence ("I +"). The expectation is that "diversification" decreases when "complexity" is bigger than "vulnerability". "Diversification" will increase until a balance (the quantities are qualitatively equal) between "vulnerability" and "complexity" is reached.

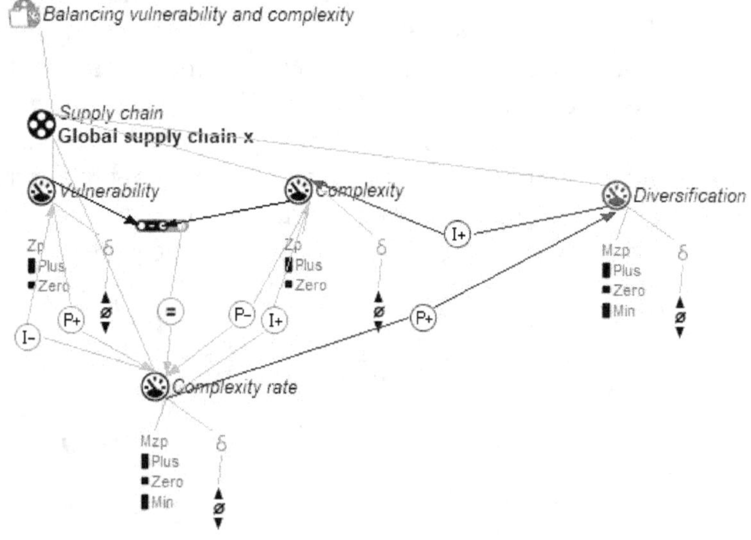

Figure 5: Rebalancing the supply chain
Source: own representation

3.4. Analysis

The purpose of this section is to analyze the simulation results. In the course of analyzing the simulation results, new perspectives can be created for decision-makers in the supply chain management field. The simulation provides a state graph of five states (Fig. 6). The path is {1-->2-->3-->4-->5}.

Figu re 6: State graph with five states
Source: own representation (Garp3)

To get information about the development of the individual quantities, the value history from Fig. 7 is used. "Drive" increases in states 1 and 2, stabilizes in state 3 and decreases in states 4 and 5. "Vulnerability" follows the development of "Drive", i.e., its stabilized in state 4. "Complexity" pursues an opposite development in the states 1 and 2 compared to the quantities "drive" and "vulnerability" and stabilizes in states 3, 4 and 5. "Diversification" has an increasing trend in states 1 and 2, stabilizing in states 3 and 4 and a downward trend in state 5. "Complexity rate" starts from the qualitative value zero and moves in the interval "Plus" from the state 2 on.

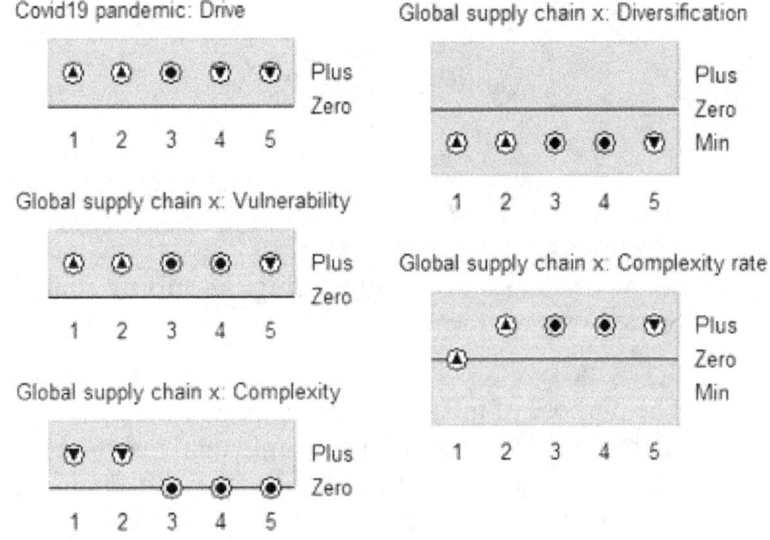

Figure 7: Value history

Source: own representation (Garp3)

4. Conclusion

The comprehensive literature research has shown that, in the author's opinion, there are six levers for more robust and thus more resilient supply chains. This research helps practitioners and decision-makers in supply chain management to identify such levers and control them in a targeted manner so that future supply chains can better react to disruptions. The six levers of robust supply chains are complexity, redundancy, flexibility, IT and digitization, regionalism, and product variety. If at least certain practices in supply chain management are reassessed, the goal of this work has been achieved. At the same time, a helpful way of thinking about systems and causal relationships in systems is presented. The conceptual models created in Garp3 force both the model creator and the model reader to think about components of a system (e.g., supply chain), their entities (e.g., suppliers and consumers) and certain quantities contained therein (e.g., service level, product variety, etc.). However, the basic statements of an interview conducted for this research show that one should not be too hopeful. The result of the Covid-19 pandemic will certainly not be a complete restructuring of the supply chains.

The topic is of the utmost relevance, especially since globalization does not end here. The aim is to conduct further expert interviews with supply chain managers and to present an even more extensive concept here.

London International Conferences, 3-5 June 2021, hosted online by UKEY Consulting and Publishing, London, United Kingdom

References

Ben-Daya, Mohamed; Hassini, Elkafi; Bahroun, Zied (2019). Internet of things and supply chain management: a literature review. International Journal of Production Research. 57 (15-16), 4719-4742, DOI: 10.1080/00207543.2017.1402140

Berger, Paul D.; Gerstenfeld, Arthur; Zeng, Amy Z. (2004). How Many Suppliers Are Best? A Decision-Analysis Approach. Omega. 32 (1), 9-15

Blackhurst, J.; Craighead, C. W. ; Elkins, D.; Handfield, R. B. (2005). An empirically derived agenda of critical research issues for managing supply-chain disruptions. International Journal of Production Research. 43 (19), 4067-4081

Bogaschewsky, Ronald (2020). Lieferketten im Stresstest – aber wollen wir wirklich die alten wiederhaben? ifo Schnelldienst. 73 (5)

Brakman, Steven; Garretsen, Harry; van Witteloostuijn, Arjen (2020). The turn from Just-in-time to Just-in-case globalization in and after times of COVID-19 - An essay on the risk re-appraisal of borders and buffers. Social Sciences & Humanities Open. 2 (1), 1-6

Bredeweg, Bert; Linnebank, Floris; Bouwer, Anders; Liem, Jochem (2009). Garp3 — Workbench for qualitative modelling and simulation. In: Ecological Informatics. 4 (5-6), 263-281. ISSN: 1574-9541

Bunde, Nicolas (2021). Covid-19 und die Industrie: Führt die Krise zum Rückbau globaler Lieferketten? ifo Schnelldienst. 74 (1), 54-57

Bundschuh, Markus; Klabjan, Diego; Thurston, Deborah L. (2003). Modeling Robust and Reliable Supply Chain, Working Paper, University of Illinois, Urbana-Champaign

Centre for Research on the Epidemiology of Disasters (2004). EM-DAT: The OFDA/ CRED International Disaster Database. Universite´ Catholique de Louvain, Brussels

Complexity Science Hub, CSH Policy Brief 06 2020. Wie robust sind die österreichischen Lieferketten? Available at https://www.csh.ac.at/csh-policy-briefs-research-briefs/

Enderwick, Peter; Buckley, Peter (2020) Rising regionalization: will the post-COVID-19 world see a retreat from globalization? Transnational Corporations. 27 (2), 99-112. DOI:10.18356/8008753a-en

Faraj, Samer; Renno, Wadih; Bhardwaj, Anand (2021). Unto the breach: What the COVID-19 pandemic exposes about digitalization. Information and Organization. 31 (1)

Fonseca, Luis Miguel; Azevedo Américo Lopes (2020). COVID- 19: outcomes for Global Supply Chains. Management & Marketing. Sciendo. 15 (s1), 424-438

Görg, Holger; Mösle, Saskia (2020). Globale Wertschöpfungsketten in Zeiten von (Und Nach) Covid 19. ifo Schnelldienst, 73 (3-7)

Gupta, Himanshu; Kumar, Sarangdhar; Kusi-Sarpong, Simonov; Jabbour, Charbel; Agyemang, Martin (2020). Enablers to supply chain performance on the basis of digitization technologies. Industrial Management and Data Systems. ahead-of-print. 10.1108/IMDS-07-2020-0421.

Hans Böckler Stiftung (2021). LIEFERKETTEN: "JE KOMPLEXER, DESTO ANFÄLLIGER". Interview with Fulda Barbara, Available at https://www.boeckler.de/de/interviews-17944-22208.htm

Institute for Supply Chain Management. COVID-19 Survey Round 3: Supply Chain Disruptions Continue Globally. Available at https://www.ismworld.org/supply-management-news-and-reports/news-publications/releases/2020/covid-19-survey-round-3-supply-chain-disruptions-continue-globally/

Jain, Nitish; Girotra, Karan; Netessine, Serguei (2020). Recovering Global Supply Chains from Sourcing Interruptions: The Role of Sourcing Strategy. INSEAD Working Paper No. 2016/58/TOM, Available at SSRN: https://ssrn.com/abstract=2682522 or http://dx.doi.org/1 0.2139/ssrn.2682522

Kim, H.M.; Laskowski, M.; Nan, N. (2018). A First Step in the Co-Evolution of Blockchain and Ontologies: Towards Engineering an Ontology of Governance at the Blockchain Protocol Level. arXiv

Liedtke, C., Kühlert, M., Wiesen, K., Stinder, A. K., Brauer, J., Beckmann, J., Fedato, C., El Mourabit, X., Büttgen, A., & Speck, M. Nachhaltige Lieferketten (Zukunftsimpuls No. 11). Wuppertal Institut, Available at https://epub.wupperinst.org/frontdoor/deliver/index/docId/7635/file/ZI11_Lieferketten.pdf

McKinsey Global Institute (2020). Risk, resilience, and rebalancing in global value chains, Available at https://www.mckinsey.com/business-functions/operations/our-insights/risk-resilience-and-rebalancing-in-global-value-chains

Nahmias, Steven; Olsen, Tava Lennon (2015). Production and Operations Analysis., Waveland Press Inc., Seventh Edition

OECD, WTO, World Band Group (2014). Global Value Chains: Challenges, Opportunities, and Implications for Policy, Available at https://www.oecd.org/

Kashmanian, Richard (2017). Building Greater Transparency in Supply Chains to Advance Sustainability. Environmental Quality Management. 26 (3), 73-104

Petersen, Thiess, Senior Advisor at Bertelsmann Stiftung, email-communication, May 16h 2021

Javorcik, Beata (2020). Global supply chains will not be the same in the post-COVID-19 world. In: COVID-19 and Trade Policy: Why Turning Inward Won't Work; Baldwin, R.E., Evenett, S.J., Eds.; CEPR Press: London, UK, 2020, 111-116

SerdarAsan, Seyda. (2013). A review of supply chain complexity drivers. Computers & Industrial Engineering. 66, 533-540, 10.1016/j.cie.2012.12.008

Sheffi, Yossi; Rice, James Blayney (2005). A Supply Chain View of the Resilient Enterprise. MIT Sloan Management Review. 47 (1), 41-48

Srinidhi, Bin; Tayi, Giri Kumar (2004). Just in time or just in case? An explanatory model with informational and incentive effects. Journal of Manufacturing Technology Management. 15 (7), 567-574

Thiele, Rainer, Director of the "Kiel Institute Africa Initiative", https://www.ifw-kiel.de/de/experten/ifw/rainer-thiele/, Telephone Interview, May 26th, 2021

Thonemann, U. W. T; Bradley, James R. (2002). The effect of product variety on supply-chain performance. European Journal of Operational Research. 143 (3), 548-569